5.99

Living
LIT

R

Hodder & Stoughton

A MEMBER OF THE HODDER HEADLINE GROUP

Acknowledgements

The publishers would like to thank the following for their kind permission to reproduce copyright material:

Text permissions:
p. 42 *A Taste of Honey* by Shelagh Delaney © Methuen Publishing.; p. 50–1 *The Crucible* by Arthur Miller copyright © 1952, 1953, 1954 by Arthur Miller. Copyright renewed 1981. Reproduced by permission of the author c/o Rogers, Coleridge & White Ltd., 20 Powis Mews, London, W11 1JN in association with International Creative Management, New York; p. 65–6 *Death of a Saleman* copyright by Arthur Miller © 1949 by Arthur Miller. Reproduced by permission of the author c/o Rogers, Coleridge & White Ltd., 20 Powis Mews, London, W11 1JN in association with International Creative Management, New York; p. 69–70 *Owbers* by Caryle Churchill © Methuen Publishing Ltd; p. 95 Review of Richard II © Evening Standard, 22 May 2000; p. 118 *Road* by Jim Cartwright © Methuen Publishing Ltd.

Copyright artwork:
p. 22 Theatre of Dionysus at Athens by J. Buhlmann © Corbis; p. 31 The Swan Playhouse by Johannes de Witt © Hulton Deutsh; p. 31 Reconstruction of phase 1 of the Rose Theatre by C. Walter Hodges © Museum of London; p. 77 *Othello*, Savoy Theatre, 1930 © Mander & Mitchenson Theatre Collection; p. 88 Christopher Marlowe © the Masters and Fellows of Corpus Christi College, Cambridge/Hulton Getty; p. 96 Samuel West as King Richard II, RSC © Donald Cooper/Photo*stage*; p. 96 Ralph Fiennes as King Richard II, Almeida Theatre 6. © Donald Cooper/Photo*stage*.

Every effort has been made to trace copyright holders of material reproduced in this book. Any rights not acknowledged will be acknowledged in subsequent printings if notice is given to the publisher.

Order queries: please contact Bookpoint Ltd, 130 Milton Park, Abingdon, Oxon OX14 4SB. Telephone: (44) 01235 827720, Fax: (44) 01235 400454. Lines are open from 9.00–6.00pm, Monday to Saturday, with a 24 hour message answering service. Email address: orders@bookpoint.co.uk

British Library Cataloguing in Publication Data
A catalogue entry for this title is available from The British Library

ISBN 0 340 79956 0

First published 2001
Impression number   10 9 8 7 6 5 4 3 2 1
Year   2007 2006 2005 2004 2003 2002 2001

Cover photo from The Ronald Grant Archive
Typeset by Fakenham Photosetting Limited, Fakenham, Norfolk
Printed in Great Britain for Hodder & Stoughton Educational, a division of Hodder Headline Plc, 338 Euston Road, London NW1 3BH by J. W. Arrowsmith Ltd, Bristol

Contents

For Claire, Mum and Dad for all their love and support.

Many thanks to my colleagues at Bolton School, particularly Ralph Britton, for being so generous with their experience, expertise and patience.

The curtain goes up and down. Something has happened. Right? Cockeyed, brutish, absurd, with no comment. Where is the comment, the slant, the explanatory note? In the play. Everything to do with the play is in the play.

(Harold Pinter, in a letter to Peter Wood, 30 March 1958)

Preface

Many students struggle when faced with the study of drama texts at AS and A Level. By now, after the rigours of GCSE, you are no doubt fairly adept at studying language and know your metaphors from your oxymorons. The problem is, the drama text is a very different kettle of fish indeed. A play doesn't contain the linguistic footholds of poetry, unless you analyse the poetry of Shakespeare's plays, say – but even then, wouldn't that be missing the point? This book intends to offer similar footholds to those of poetry and prose, so that you don't find your journey through drama too slippery, by focusing on both the **skills** needed to approach a drama text and the **knowledge** of such surrounding factors as history, contexts and interpretations.

Speaking of Shakespeare, a quick glance at the contents will reveal that his name is conspicuous in its absence, something which may seem odd considering he is the only dramatist you will all study. This isn't some horrendous administrative error (in fact he does actually appear in every chapter – far more than any other dramatist) but rather, this being a book about *drama* rather than a book about authors, it seemed a far better idea to stick to themes and to consider Shakespeare as one dramatist among many – albeit a particularly impressive and famous one. There is a chapter devoted to him in the original *Living Literature* textbook; otherwise, the so-called 'Shakespeare Industry' is thriving well enough without me adding to it.

Finally, remember that unlike poetry and prose, drama was never intended to be read in a classroom, but to be seen in performance. As a result, many of the activities in the book focus on recreating the *performance context* of the work by encouraging dramatic reading and performances. Don't feel embarrassed – performing the scripts is an essential part of appreciating them, even if acting isn't to Oscar-winning standards. If you get the chance, experience if not *your* set texts then at least *a* text, in performance. It will give you a valuable insight into much of the drama in this book. You may also enjoy it.

R. G. 2001

1 The Properties of Drama

In this chapter, you will investigate drama as a form of literature, and consider the properties it has which are similar to, and different from, poetry and prose.

'Dramatic' texts

What exactly do we mean when we talk about a text being 'dramatic'? The word is used nowadays to mean many different things in different situations. Newspapers use it on an almost daily basis: we may hear of a politician's 'dramatic intervention', or a prisoner's 'dramatic reprieve'; goalkeepers can make 'dramatic saves' just as firemen can make a 'dramatic rescue', and television companies make much of the programmes they produce labelled 'Drama', as opposed to documentaries or comedies.

However, the word is not just a modern one. As early as the fourth century BC, the Greek philosopher Aristotle was using the word in his *Poetics*, describing the drama (meaning 'a thing done', from the Greek verb *dran*, 'to do'), of the time as

A representation of an action that is worth serious attention, complete in itself, and of some amplitude ... the representation not only of a complete action, but also of incidents that awaken fear and pity, and effects of this kind are heightened when things happen unexpectedly as well as logically, for then they will be more remarkable than if they seem merely mechanical or accidental.

It may be that you yourself have some experience of drama as a school subject – which probably means acting of some kind. How, then, does the idea of sitting down to study a text – as some would with a novel or a poem – relate to all these different ideas of drama?

ACTIVITY 1

Key skills: communication – discussion

1 Individually, rank order the list below going from what you consider to be the least (6) to the most (1) dramatic. As you are doing so, think about why you consider one thing to be more dramatic than another. Do the different situations provoke different reactions? Do they have different kinds of 'drama' in them?

1 soap opera
2 sports match
3 an argument between friends
4 the news
5 a costume/period drama (eg the television adaptation of 'Pride and Prejudice')

6 Shakespeare
2 Now compare your list with that of the person next to you in class. Explain your choices to each other and agree on a new, revised list. Then from this list, try to create a definition in one or two sentences, of what you consider 'dramatic' to mean.

3 Now report your results back to the class and try to agree a new, class definition.
4 Compare your class definition to Aristotle's. Are there any similarities? Differences?

COMMENTARY No doubt you had many different ideas about what the pecking order of the list should have been, and for very different reasons. Perhaps you had a vague idea that Shakespeare should have been top, without really knowing why or necessarily considering it the most dramatic. This was probably because your cultural knowledge was telling you one thing, but your personal experience was suggesting something else. You may react to an argument between friends, for example, because it has a direct relevance and so directly engages your interest. Perhaps a soap opera was second because, although fictional, it deals with issues you recognise and understand.

However, we have to draw a definite distinction between drama as something which engages our emotions because it happens in real life, and drama as something which is fictional and consciously crafted. Passionate as you may feel about a dispute between friends, the argument itself may be almost incomprehensible to an outside party, being little more than a string of references to people, places and incidents only your close circle would know. Even if this were not the case, the conversation may well be full of stutters, interruptions and repetition, as all conversations tend to be, which would probably reduce its impact to an outsider as they struggled to understand the high-speed exchange. In short, it would not have been created to have what we could call an *objective emotional impact* – to have roughly the same effect on a number of people unconnected with the incident.

It is here that your definitions may have differed from those of Aristotle. Notice that he places emphasis on the crafted aspects of Greek Tragedy (see Chapter 3): drama for him is 'the *representation* of an action, *complete in itself.*' Real life, of course, is not 'complete in itself'; it has no such careful structure and isn't selective in what it displays. However, drama as a literary *genre* does and is. It is important that we always keep this idea in our minds when reading dramatic texts. They aren't transcripts of real conversations, however authentic. They are illusions created by writers who have a point to make. This illusion of reality on the stage we call *verisimilitude* – something we have to be on our guard against, because it makes us forget drama is a form of literature just as carefully created as poetry or prose. In fact, some dramatists (such as Brecht – see Chapter 5) deliberately use techniques to prevent this happening, as they feel it is important that the audience is constantly aware of the crafted nature of what they are viewing.

Poetry, Prose and Drama: Three Example Texts

Key skills: communication: reading/discussion

Below are two text extracts and one complete work. They have been chosen from each of the main literary genres; poetry, prose and drama.

At the end of each extract is a series of questions to stimulate some thought before you move on to the next. Spend some time reading them and then note down your comments on the texts, using the questions as a guide to your ideas.

Text A: The opening of *Wuthering Heights* by Emily Brontë

1801 – I have just returned from a visit to my landlord – the solitary neighbour that I shall be troubled with. This is certainly a beautiful country! In all England, I do not believe that I could have fixed on a situation so completely removed from the stir of society. A perfect misanthropist's Heaven – and Mr Heathcliff and I are such a suitable pair to divide the desolation between us. A capital fellow! He little imagined how my heart warmed towards him when I beheld his little black eyes withdraw so suspiciously under their brows, as I rode up, and when his fingers sheltered themselves, with a jealous resolution, still further in his waistcoat, as I announced my name.

'Mr Heathcliff?' I said.

A nod was the answer.

'Mr Lockwood, your new tenant, sir. I do myself the honour of calling as soon as possible, after my arrival, to express the hope that I have not inconvenienced you by my perseverance in soliciting the occupation of Thrushcross Grange: I heard, yesterday, you had had some thoughts –'

'Thrushcross Grange is my own, sir,' he interrupted wincing, 'I should not allow anyone to inconvenience me, if I could hinder it – walk in!'

The 'walk in' was uttered with closed teeth, and expressed the sentiment, 'Go to the Deuce'; even the gate over which he leant manifested no sympathizing movement to the words; and I think that circumstances determined me to accept the invitation: I felt interested in a man who seemed more exaggeratedly reserved than myself.

When he saw my horse's breast fairly pushing the barrier, he did pull out his hand to unchain it, and then sullenly preceded me up the causeway, calling, as we entered the court:

'Joseph, take Mr Lockwood's horse; and bring up some wine.'

'Here we have the whole establishment of domestics, I suppose,' was the reflection, suggested by this compound order. 'No wonder the grass grows between the flags, and cattle are the only hedge-cutters.'

Joseph was an elderly, nay, an old man, though very hale and sinewy.

'The Lord help us!' He soliloquised in an undertone of peevish displeasure, while relieving me of my horse: looking, meantime, in my face so sourly that I charitably conjectured he must have need of divine aid to digest his dinner, and his pious ejaculation had no reference to my unexpected advent.

Wuthering Heights is the name of Mr Heathcliff's dwelling, 'Wuthering' being a significant provincial adjective, descriptive of the atmospheric tumult to which its station is exposed in stormy weather. Pure, bracing ventilation they must have up there at all times, indeed: one may guess the power of the north wind, blowing over the edge, by the excessive slant of a few stunted firs at the end of the house; and by a range of gaunt thorns all stretching their limbs one way, as if craving alms of the sun. Happily, the architect had foresight to build it strong: the narrow windows are deeply set into the wall, and the corners defended by large jutting stones.

Ask yourself the following questions about this text:

- How important is the narrator in this opening? For example, what role does he play in the action? What extra information does he provide?
- How much of this opening is action, and how much is thought/ideas? Think about other novels you have read. How typical is this extract of a prose style?
- How easy would it be to dramatise this opening?
- The extract opens with a date – '1801'. What does this suggest to us about the style and content of the writing which will follow?

Text B: *Composed upon Westminster Bridge, September 3 1802* by William Wordsworth

Earth has not anything to show more fair:
Dull would he be of soul who could pass by
A sight so touching in its majesty:
This City now doth, like a garment, wear
The beauty of the morning; silent, bare,
Ships, towers, domes, theatres and temples lie
Open unto the fields, and to the sky;
All bright and glittering in the smokeless air.
Never did sun more beautifully steep
In his first splendour, valley, rock or hill;
Ne'er saw I, never felt, a calm so deep!
The river glideth at his own sweet will:
Dear God! The very houses seem asleep;
And all that mighty heart is lying still!

Here are some questions to ask yourself about this text:

- Is there a narrator of any kind in this poem? What purpose does the poem serve?
- Is there any kind of narrative in this poem?
- How many typically 'poetic' devices can you find in the poem?
- What is the writer's purpose in this poem?

Text C: from Act II, scene ii of *School for Scandal* by Richard Sheridan

(Mrs Candour, Crabtree, Sir Benjamin Backbite, Joseph Surface, Lady Teazle and Maria have met at the house of the local socialite Mrs Sneerwell. They have just been 'admiring' some verses written by Sir Benjamin.)

Enter LADY TEAZLE and MARIA

MRS CANDOUR: I must have a copy.
LADY SNEERWELL: Lady Teazle, I hope we shall see Sir Peter.
LADY TEAZLE: I believe he'll wait on your ladyship – presently.
LADY SNEERWELL: Maria, my love, you look grave. Come, you shall sit down to cards with Mr Surface.
MARIA: I take very little pleasure in cards – however, I'll do as your ladyship pleases.
LADY TEAZLE: *(aside)* I am surprised Mr Surface should sit down with her – I thought he would have embraced this opportunity of speaking to me before Sir Peter came.
MRS CANDOUR: *(coming forward)*: Now I'll die, but you are so scandalous I'll forswear your society.
LADY TEAZLE: What's the matter, Mrs Candour?
MRS CANDOUR: They'll not allow our friend Miss Vermilion to be handsome.
LADY SNEERWELL: O surely she's a pretty woman.
CRABTREE: I am very glad you think so, Ma'am.

MRS CANDOUR: She has a charming fresh colour.

LADY TEAZLE: Yes, when it is fresh put on.

MRS CANDOUR: O fie! I'll swear her colour is natural – I have seen it come and go.

LADY TEAZLE: I dare swear you have, Ma'am – it goes of a night and comes again in the morning.

MRS CANDOUR: Ha! Ha! Ha! How I hate to hear you talk so! But surely now her sister is, or was, very handsome.

CRABTREE: Who? Mrs Evergreen? – O Lord, she's six and fifty if she's an hour!

MRS CANDOUR: Now positively you wrong her; fifty-two or fifty-three is the utmost – and I don't think she looks more.

SIR BENJAMIN: Ah! There is no judging by her looks unless one could see her face.

LADY SNEERWELL: Well, well, if Mrs Evergreen does take some pains to repair the ravages of time, you must allow she effects it with great ingenuity – and surely that's better than the careless manner in which the widow Ochre caulks her wrinkles.

SIR BENJAMIN: Nay, now, Lady Sneerwell, you are severe upon the widow. Come, come, it is not that she paints so ill – but when she has finished her face, she joins it on so badly to her neck that she looks like a mended statue, in which the connoisseur sees at once that the head's modern, though the trunk's antique.

CRABTREE: Ha! Ha! Ha! Well said, nephew!

MRS CANDOUR: Ha! Ha! Ha! Well, you make me laugh but I vow I hate you for it. – What do you think of Miss Simper?

SIR BENJAMIN: Why, she has very pretty teeth.

LADY TEAZLE: Yes, and on that account, when she is neither speaking nor laughing (which very seldom happens), she never absolutely shuts her mouth but leaves it always on a jar as it were.

MRS CANDOUR: How can you be so ill-natured?

Think about the following questions:

- Is there evidence of an author or narrator of any sorts in this extract?
- Which of the characters do we like or dislike, if any? Why? Does this suggest anything about the author's purpose?
- How might the 'asides' be played? What purpose do they serve?

ACTIVITY 3

Key skills: communication – reading/discussion

1 In groups, discuss and then list in a table the aspects of each text which you feel are representative of its form. For example, you might list the rhyme in Wordsworth's poem as a distinctive feature.

Prose	Poetry	Drama
Wuthering Heights	*Composed upon Westminster Bridge . . .*	*School for Scandal*
	Rhyme	

Don't be too choosy: list as many as you can, including visual features. You probably knew which was which before you even began reading because of their layout. Does this tell us anything?

2 Now, still in groups, look across the completed list and see if there are any crossover features – again, rhyme certainly appears in poetry, but is it exclusive to it? Place a tick next to any features that cross over. You should be left with a clear number of features distinctive to that form only (if there are any!).

3 Next, discuss the results as a class and reach an agreement about the distinctive features of the three texts.

ACTIVITY 4

Key skills: communication – discussion
Now look particularly at the extract from
Wuthering Heights. Imagine that you have been
commissioned to write a dramatic version of the
story for the stage. You must decide on the
opening of the play and adapt it from the novel.
In groups, discuss the way in which you will
adapt it. Think about such things as:

- The way the stage will look – how are you
  going to convey the wild conditions
  described by the narrator?
- The way you are going to introduce the
  characters in the opening.
- Whether or not you are going to tamper
  with the dialogue. Will you create more or
  less?

ACTIVITY 5

**Key skills: communication – writing
documents/presentation**

In your groups, write the adaptation and take
turns to perform it. Then, as a class, offer
feedback on each version and discuss the

decisions you had to make. Focus on your
difficulties in adapting the story to the stage;
this will give you practical experience of the
very distinctive aspects of theatre which can be
overlooked when reading a dramatic text.

COMMENTARY

No doubt a number of issues became apparent as you compared the three
different texts. It may be that you struggled to find neat distinctions
between the forms of literature, probably because they don't really exist.
Believe it or not, writers through the ages didn't produce literature for the
benefit of students and teachers! As a result, literature rarely arrives in neat
packets and almost any assertion we make about a text can be disproved by
an exception to the rule.

For example, you may have identified *narrative* as a major aspect of prose –
that is, it tells a story. But then, drama clearly also gives us a visual story –
and what about poetry? A lyric such as Wordsworth's in Text B doesn't,
but then *narrative* poetry such as *Paradise Lost* by John Milton clearly does.
We have to beware of generalisations – or at least, to know we are using
them if that is the case. With that warning in mind, there are some general
points that we can make about the texts:

Wuthering Heights and the narrative voice

The major difference you should have noticed between the extract from
Wuthering Heights and the other two is the presence of a distinctive
narrative voice – that is, a voice which tells us the story, commenting and
amplifying on the action; giving opinions and insights. In the case of
Wuthering Heights, the narrative is *first person* – that is, the narrator is a
character in the novel. We are given his thoughts, feelings and reactions to
other characters and our view of the action is through his/her eyes.
However, because such narrators are characters in the novel as well, their
viewpoint is limited to their own ideas and feelings. *Third person narrative*
– where the narrator is not a character, but an outside agent viewing the
action – can go even further, with the narrator probing into the minds and
thoughts of different characters, revealing important (and, in some cases,
otherwise unknown) information in an almost 'god-like' way. This does

not necessarily mean the narrative is unbiased – the narrator often takes the perspective of one specific character and so guides our reactions to events.

In *Wuthering Heights* the narrative voice is very distinctive – fluent and eloquent, but rather too much so it seems, in the society in which he finds himself. His 'solitary neighbour', he tells us, withdraws his 'black eyes' suspiciously and barely even speaks, and when he does it is with a 'wince'. The date at the opening suggests this is a diary and the narrator, Lockwood, talks directly to us in a friendly and conversational manner, as one would write in a diary, so that he almost becomes like a character in the novel. Notice how many reflections and opinions are given – 'This is certainly a beautiful country!'; 'A capital fellow!' – as well as general information on the environment – 'the power of the north wind ...'. This is the kind of information we might expect in a personal diary, which the opening date suggests it is meant to be.

It is here your difficulties may have arisen in translating the passage into a stage performance. Should Lockwood be a character, like all others, which would presumably mean he couldn't talk directly to the audience? Or should he be a narrating figure, standing aloof from the action and commenting on it? If you opted for the latter, then it was a significant choice; you have rejected so-called realistic theatre and instead chosen a form which breaks the conventional rules of what we expect to happen in real life. It might be, as a compromise, that you decided to portray a character writing a diary, talking to himself while others acted the events behind him; but even here you have taken liberties, playing around with time – the past and the present can't exist at the same time!

Wordsworth's Sonnet

Wordsworth's poem certainly has a 'voice' in that it describes one person's reaction to the sight of London in the morning. There is no real *narrative* to the poem, however, except the incident which created the composition itself – that is, that the writer happened to be on Westminster Bridge, arrested by the sight of London, so much so he wanted to write about it. This gives the impression of a spontaneous reaction – Wordsworth himself described poetry as 'the spontaneous overflow of powerful emotion', which this poem appears to be. However, the poem itself is carefully wrought. It is a sonnet, with a particularly intricate rhyme scheme (abbaabbacdcdcd). The poem focuses on description, both of London and the poet's response to it, and, if pleasure is to be gained from it (if we can assume that is one of the purposes of literature), it is from the quality of the description Wordsworth uses to convey the atmosphere – the simile of the 'garment' of the morning and the 'silent, bare' aspects of the city he views – and the strength of the poet's reaction to it.

Sheridan's *School for Scandal*

However, the extract from *School for Scandal* has nothing similar to either of these clear, 'controlling' voices. There is the 'italic voice' (if we can call it that) that reveals who is speaking and, occasionally, *how* they speak, but that is all – and, of course, this is something only an actor or a reader is aware of. In performance, it is up to the actor to convey the instructions given by this 'italic' voice. Unless (as you may have done in your adaptation of *Wuthering Heights*) a narrator is used, the characters speak and behave for themselves. In many ways, authors have far less control over their material.

This is the important difference between the piece of prose and the poem, and the dramatic extract. The *Wuthering Heights* extract and the Wordsworth poem are completed works of art. They will now always stay the same (although open to different interpretations – see Chapter 5). However, the drama script is only partly completed: it can only be fully realised in a performance; and, of course, every performance will be slightly different, even though the actors are bound by the words on the page.

We are also disadvantaged in our reactions to these characters, as we are in real life, by the fact that we are not aware of the motives and thoughts behind their behaviour. In this scene, our only insight into any such thoughts is through the *aside*, in this case demonstrating Lady Teazle's jealousy. This is a dramatic convention in which characters speak to themselves and the audience, unheard by other characters in the play. This is one of the ways in which a playwright can convey on the stage things we may take for granted in a novel.

ACTIVITY 6

1 What other ways are there in which authors can influence the audience's reactions to a play? List as many as you can! (You will find a suggested list at the end of the chapter.)

2 The 'asides' suggest an author at work in some way in the extract, allowing us some insight into the characters' behaviour. You should have been able to feel yourself being 'pushed' in a particular direction as you were reading the extract, even though there was no direct comment. This has been termed the 'implied author' – although not apparent, we can feel an over-riding influence in the scene. We are clearly meant to see the gossip and backbiting in the scene in a negative light. We can see, in the extract, that Mrs Candour is an absurd and rather nasty character, pretending to be horrified by other characters' comments when she is actually enjoying them. The very names of the characters imply the presence of an author, suggestive as they are of their personalities: 'Sneerwell', 'Backbite', and (ironically) 'Candour'. Maria, the one sympathetic character in the scene, is strangely quiet and inept in such company. How might an actor portray Maria in this scene to make her discomfort clear to the audience?

So, we have considered some of the aspects which make drama unique as a literary genre. You have even had some practical play writing experience. However, there is still one very important introductory aspect to consider before we move on.

Staging

**Key skills: communication –
writing/presentation/discussion**

1 On your own, write a description of the last
time you went to the theatre. It doesn't
necessarily have to have been a
straightforward play; it may have been a
musical. Try to write down chronologically
all of the things that had an effect on you
from the moment you entered the
auditorium.
2 Share your ideas with the class and produce a
class list of all the different aspects of theatre
which can influence or affect an audience.

Works of prose and poetry convey meaning on their own terms but, as we
have seen, drama scripts are written to be performed and so are bound by
the number of specific difficulties involved in performance. Not least of
these are aspects of staging: in other words, the practicalities of where the
play is to be performed and to what kind of an audience. In the list you
produced for the last activity, no doubt such things as set (the scenery on
the stage), costume, lighting and music all have an important part to play
(pardon the pun) in its appearance as a finished product. Similarly, the
words on the page are also brought to life with the inclusion of a variety of
different movements, facial expressions and tones of voice by the individual
actors who interpret the role. All of these aspects of performance which we
do not find in the written words of the playscript are known as *stage
business*.

Of course, the playwright is able to influence aspects of stage business
through the use of *stage directions*. You have no doubt been reading stage
directions from the first time you ever read a play and, as a result, it is easy
to take them for granted and even gloss over them as a minor irritation in
our reading. However, they can perform very different functions depending
upon the type of play and the playwright and they can reveal a considerable
amount about the author's intentions for the play in performance – which
of course is where the play will come alive. Some of the different purposes
of stage directions are:

■ to suggest movement or action
■ to indicate set, staging and sound requirements
■ to suggest how an actor should say a particular line
■ to express what a character is thinking or feeling at any particular
  moment
■ to offer any other advice as to interpretation of character and set,
  including reference to possible symbolism.

Shakespeare was notorious for the scarcity of his stage directions, whereas
modern writers such as Arthur Miller and Tennessee Williams tend to
provide far more detailed and demanding instructions (for the openings of
two of their plays, see Chapter 3). Here is an example of some opening set
instructions, taken from Bill Naughton's *Spring and Port Wine*:

SCENE: *The living room, kitchen and scullery of the Crompton home. Early Friday evening.*
Most of the stage is taken up by the living room, which has a bay window down right, a door to the hall up centre and one to the kitchen up left. The kitchen also has a door in its downstage wall which leads to the scullery. The scullery extends down left of the living room wall, and in its own left wall is the back door of the house. The front door is off up right of the corridor centre. The house is a comfortable, prosperous, working class home. The furniture is fairly modern, everything is polished and well cared for. There is nothing cheap and vulgar.

These instructions are fairly straightforward. However, even here there may be a number of terms in this opening which you are not familiar with, particularly those which relate to the geography of the rooms. 'Down right', 'up centre', 'up left', 'downstage' – all of these phrases refer to the position of various parts of the set and have a specific meaning. Phrases like 'down left' and 'downstage' in fact refer to the orientation of objects from the perspective of the actors; so 'stage left' and 'stage right' would be opposite to the audience's left and right, and 'upstage' is the part of the stage furthest from the audience (to 'upstage' someone is to push them away from the audience, to the back of the stage area). There is clearly a vocabulary of the stage which playwrights and actors are familiar with.

TERMINOLOGY BOX 1

Wings: the areas at either side of the stage where actors wait just before they are to come on.

Footlights: fairly obviously, lights which sit at the very front of the stage.

Backstage: the area behind the stage where actors wait and prepare.

Apron: the part of the stage which juts out in front of the curtain.

Orchestra: the area between the stage and the audience, sometimes referred to as the 'pit' because it is lower than the stage so that the musicians are out of sight of the audience.

These all refer to areas in a traditional, or *proscenium*, theatre, the one you are probably used to, where the audience sits in rows facing in one direction, facing a (usually raised) stage where the actors perform in a space under a large arch, rather like a large version of a Punch and Judy show. This is clearly what Bill Naughton had in mind for *Spring and Port Wine*.

ACTIVITY 8

Key skills: communication – discussion/writing documents

Based on Bill Naughton's stage directions, draw a plan of the stage as it would appear in a proscenium arch production of *Spring and Port Wine*. As well as drawing aspects of set, indicate areas of the stage 'geography' using the terms you have been given – upstage, downstage and so on.

Although most common since the nineteenth century, the proscenium theatre is not the only way a play can be staged. Other ways are:

- Thrust stage – the stage literally thrusts out into the audience, so some members of the audience are seated at the sides of the stage;
- Traverse stage – the audience sits on either side of the stage which is in the middle of the auditorium;
- 'In the Round' – where the audience sits in a circle (or similar shape) all the way around the stage;
- Promenade – there is no distinct difference between the stage and audience. The audience stands and often the action takes place around it.

Figure 1 shows these ways of seating the audience in relation to the stage. Some are new, but some are very old – the 'thrust stage' was in fact the type of stage Shakespeare's plays would originally have been seen on. Of course, the playwright's intentions are not always necessarily heeded – although he had clearly been thinking of a proscenium stage, Naughton's *Spring and Port Wine* was recently performed 'in the round' in his native Bolton.

ACTIVITY 9

1 Look at each of the possible stage layouts in Figure 1 and list the advantages and disadvantages of them for
   a) an audience
   b) actors.
2 What considerations would a director have to make in deciding which layout to use? What problems would s/he face for each?
3 Are any particular stage styles appropriate for specific plays?

4 Choose a play you know well and then decide which of the stage layouts you think would work best with it. For example, if your play contains a scene with a large crowd, then a promenade performance may work quite well. When you have chosen the stage type, share your ideas with a partner, justifying your choice.

COMMENTARY

The proscenium stage usually places some distance between the actors and audience, whereas 'in the round' and the traverse stage create a far more intimate tone, as often the audience is very close to the action – but this can also make more demands on the actors! Sometimes the actors actually use the intimacy to their advantage: in a recent production of *Much Ado About Nothing*, Josie Lawrence caused havoc by attempting to hide in the front row! In a proscenium or thrust stage, the audience is all facing in one direction only which makes it easier for the actors to make sure everything they do can be seen. However, 'in the round' seems more natural despite causing difficulties in terms of what is called 'blocking' (making sure that actors stand in such a way that they do not obscure any of the audience's view), rather than the slightly artificial acting required by the proscenium stage. Entrances and exits are more obviously fixed with a proscenium stage, whereas productions with the audience surrounding the stage can allow for more flexibility – or cause more problems, depending on how you look at it! Ultimately, it is up to an individual director to decide which

Proscenium Stage

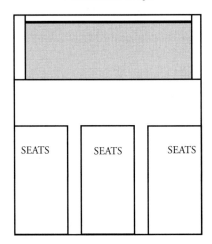

Thrust Stage

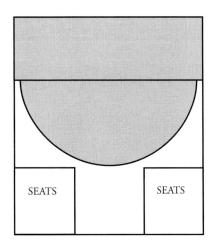

Traverse Stage

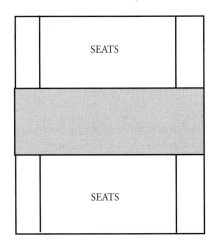

'In the Round'

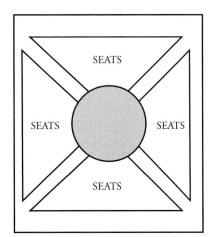

Promenade

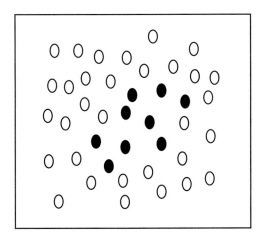

stage will suit the particular production, which will obviously also depend on the constraints of the theatre itself. All the stage types have advantages and disadvantages and all affect the way in which the text will be presented.

'Drama' and 'Theatricality'

What should by now be clear is that drama is a very different literary genre to poetry or prose, in that it is only ever fully realised in performance, and so it is important for us to consider the *dramatic implications* of the text; in other words, what kind of effect the drama would have on an audience. However, it is also important to distinguish between *dramatic* devices and *theatrical* devices. A dramatic device exists in the written text; a theatrical device exists in the performance. As you will see in the next chapter, the history of dramatic literature is very uneven, precisely because at certain times in its history audiences were more interested in *theatrical* elements – such as set, staging and special effects – than with dramatic aspects such as character, theme and dialogue and, of course, audiences were given what they wanted. For example, much of the drama of the nineteenth century, particularly the sub-genre known as *melodrama,* holds little interest for literature students because the script itself was less important than aspects of theatre which drew attention away from the content of the play. As a result, the quality of much nineteenth-century drama as literature is inferior to that of, say, Renaissance drama in the early seventeenth century. As literature students, you should consider the way a dramatist has exploited aspects of staging, whilst focusing clearly on important aspects of the text as a work of literature, i.e. on your interpretation of meaning, character and theme as it will appear in performance.

Reading Drama Texts at AS and A Level and how this book can help you

Clearly, then, the dramatic text has a number of aspects which are very different from the 'normal' text you would approach at AS or A Level. It is not enough just to talk about characters and themes as you would with a novel, although these remain important. When your work is being assessed, the examiners will be looking for a specific number of skills – known as the **assessment objectives**. It is worth briefly considering what these are, how they will relate to your study of plays, and how they will be dealt with in this book. A candidate who goes into an examination without a real idea of what the examiners want is clearly at a severe disadvantage.

The assessment objectives (AOs) are as follows:
AO1: **communicate clearly the knowledge, understanding and insight appropriate to literary study, using appropriate terminology and accurate and written expression.**
This obviously relates to your ability to write accurately and fluently, a skill necessary to all texts; however, it also makes reference to 'appropriate

terminology' – using the specific terms relevant to the form you are studying. Drama has a number of very specific terms associated with it, some of which we have already met in this chapter. Where appropriate you will find a 'terminology box' which revises any new, specific terms which have been used and which you may find useful.

AO2 i (for AS): **respond with knowledge and understanding to literary texts of different types and periods,** (plus ii at A Level) **exploring and commenting on relationships and comparisons between literary texts.**
The texts your teacher chooses from your syllabus will be 'of different types and periods', and 'knowledge and understanding' refers to clear understanding of the texts and also knowledge of any aspects which are important to that understanding. Chapter 2 of this book will provide more general background information, including a brief history of drama, enabling you to see any text you study in relation to drama as a whole. Chapter 3 will offer the opportunity to read a large number of extracts, giving examples of texts from 'different types and periods'.

AO3: **show detailed understanding of the ways in which writers' choices of form, structure and language shape meanings.**
This refers to your ability to see the text as a consciously crafted art form and to have the knowledge and skills to 'unpick' the techniques by which writers create effects. There are a number of such techniques unique to texts performed on the stage and Chapter 3 will help you explore them and provide you with the skills to do the same with any dramatic text.

AO4: **articulate independent opinions and judgments, informed by different interpretations of literary texts by other readers.**
Chapter 5 will look at aspects of interpretation that are specific to drama – for example, the role of actors and directors in interpreting the text for performance – as well as giving you some practice in forming your own interpretations and considering those of others, giving specific case studies.

AO5 i (AS): **show understanding of the contexts in which literary texts are written and understood;**
ii (at A Level): **evaluate the significance of cultural, historical and other contextual influences on literary texts and study.**
The 'contexts' of a play are the wider influencing factors which can affect the production – and reception – of literary texts. Chapter 4 will explore what some of these factors are and will examine them in action in two case studies of specific plays.

This book, then, follows the Assessment Objectives very clearly in its structure and approach, with the exception of Chapters 4 and 5 where context is considered before interpretation (the opposite of AOs 4 and 5). As you will see, in dramatic texts this is because context can often affect interpretation. Where the AOs are different for AS and A Level, the chapters offer separate activities which can provide for both, with the early chapters concentrating on range and skills, and the later chapters moving on to focus on whole texts. This will, of course, be what you will have to do in your study of drama.

COMMENTARY
To Activity 6

The following methods are open to a playwright to use to influence an audience:

- *asides;*
- *soliloquies* (in which characters speak to themselves at length on stage);
- presentation of other characters' opinions of them. Sometimes, minor characters are introduced solely for this purpose and are known as *choric figures*; sometimes major characters serve a *choric purpose* during the play. An example of the former from Shakespeare is the 'Gentleman' in *King Lear*, who appears to describe Cordelia to us and then vanishes; a Shakespearean example of the latter is Enobarbus in *Antony and Cleopatra*, whose famous speech beginning 'The barge she sat on, like a burnished throne' persuades us as to the beauty of Cleopatra;
- *juxtaposition* of scenes for satirical effect or to show the character behaving in different ways. For example, the villain Edmund in *King Lear*, who is humble and polite in front of others in the play's opening scene, reveals his true motives in a soliloquy when he is alone on stage in the next scene;
- *irony*. A character condemns himself by the foolishness or hypocrisy of what he is saying; something which becomes *dramatic irony* if the audience is aware of the hypocrisy. This technique figures very strongly in the extract from Sheridan's *School for Scandal*.
- through *stage directions* which suggest how characters should be performed, giving indications as to whether they should be sympathetic (that is, likeable) characters.

Chapter review

In this chapter, you have identified the ways in which drama differs from poetry and prose, and you have had practical experience in adapting a prose extract for the stage. You have considered the practical aspects of drama, such as performance, set and staging.

2 Backgrounds to Drama

In this chapter, you will learn about some of the literary contexts for drama, by considering the major traditions and conventions of theatre.

'Literary texts are produced by people interested in literature.'

This statement may seem obvious to the point of being absurd, but nevertheless makes an important point. Writers don't produce their works of art in a bubble, but are instead influenced by other pieces of literature and, as a result, tend to follow certain traditions, conventions and ideas (consciously or unconsciously) depending on their interests and the period in which they are writing. These influences could be described as *literary* (the influence of other types of texts, usually consciously) or *historical* (where the influence has more to do with the period the writer lived in). Sometimes, writers become part of wider *literary movements* – groups of writers who choose to do something specific, usually different to what has already gone before.

This means that when we study a play for A Level, it is important to understand it in its *literary context* (for a wider discussion of contexts, see Chapter 4). This means considering the traditions it fits into and, more importantly, how it fits into them (if it does at all). This chapter will help your knowledge and understanding of drama by considering:

i) *Genre*: the different types of drama, focusing particularly on tragedy.
ii) *The History of Drama*: a quick survey of the main periods in the history of English drama, offering examples of texts from the different periods and providing, where relevant, opportunities for wider reading.

Obviously in such a short space, the discussion of these aspects cannot pretend to be complete. For more detailed information, look to the 'Further Reading' section at the end of this book.

The Importance of *Genre*

In the previous chapter drama, poetry and prose were referred to as *genres* of literature. But what exactly does this mean? The *Concise Oxford Dictionary of Literary Terms* defines *genre*, a French term deriving from the Latin for 'species', as a recognizable and established category of written work employing such common conventions as will prevent readers or audiences from mistaking it for another kind.

In this sense, poetry, prose and drama are literary genres in that they have a number of recognizable conventions (which we considered in the last chapter). However, as with any species, they can then be broken down further into different sub-species, or sub-genres – that is, works within these three genres which themselves have 'recognizable and established' conventions. When a group of actors arrives at the palace in *Hamlet*, Polonius describes them as being 'the best actors in the world, either for tragedy, comedy, history, pastoral, pastoral-comical, historical-pastoral, tragical-comical-historical-pastoral, scene individable, or poem unlimited' – quite a large number of sub-species! Obviously, the number of different genres Polonius mentions here is absurd (Polonius is an absurd figure), but nevertheless sub-species do exist. A useful modern analogy for this is film.

ACTIVITY 10

Key skills: communication – discussion

The following activity will give you a sense of genre in action.

1 Working on your own, take a mental stroll down an aisle in your local video shop and try to remember as many film titles as you can. Jot them down and then decide if there are any recognisable film genres.

2 In pairs, share your ideas with a partner. Were there any that they had which you didn't?
3 Now focus in on one or two types of film. What are the conventions of the genre? Does the film use them subtly, or does the film draw attention to them for specific reasons? What purpose do the conventions serve?

COMMENTARY

Some of the more obvious film genres are:

- horror/scary movie
- weepie
- (spaghetti) Western
- comedy
- sci-fi
- action film.

The conventions of these sub-genres are fairly obvious. The horror movie has perhaps the most clichéd conventions of all – such as the haunted house; the innocent girl (who always returns to the haunted house alone at midnight, whatever we tell her); the disbelieving parents, etc. *Spoofs* (or, in literary terms, *parodies*) of genres demonstrate how deeply ingrained these conventions are, as they often exploit well-worn conventions for comic effect. The recent film *Scream* parodied all the classic 'rules' of the scary movie while creating a sub-sub-genre of its own, the 'teen-slasher flick'. Sometimes, films make use of conventions and devices by drawing attention to them (a technique known as 'baring the device' – see Chapter 5). For example, the scene in which the innocent but foolish girl returns to the haunted house may exploit the audience's awareness that something is going to happen by having a number of false alarms, by having brooms fall out of cupboards etc., in order to raise the audience's tension. Conventions are not something used unconsciously – they are often deliberately chosen and sometimes exploited for effect.

Key skills: communication – discussion

Now repeat the previous Activity, but this time with literature (and, in particular, drama). Consider:

1 Are there any conventions you know of? What do they add to our appreciation?
2 Which genre, poetry, prose or drama, relies most heavily on the use of sub-genre? Why do you think this is?

COMMENTARY

As a literary genre, drama is perhaps most susceptible to conventions for a variety of possible reasons. Poetry and prose are very personal forms, usually read privately by an individual. Perhaps because a number of people collaborate to produce a finished performance or perhaps because the audience makes it a greater social event, and certainly because in performance it is at the mercy of whatever resources are available in its staging, by-and-large drama has always followed clearly defined trends, rules and ideas.

The main two genres within drama are tragedy and comedy. Although comedy has often been by far the favourite genre with audiences (for obvious reasons), often it has been the writers of tragedy – tragedians – who have produced the most famous literature, probably because the seriousness of the genre encourages deeper thought and ideas. This is not to say that comedy does not have a literary value: a number of writers have pointed out that, in actual fact, comedy can have serious concerns. However, much comedy through the ages has been for purely theatrical entertainment and, although there is certainly nothing wrong with that, it has been tragedy which has stimulated the most thought. When Aristotle wrote about Ancient Greek drama in his *Poetics* (see Chapter 1), it was tragedy he was talking about; and although much admired for his comedies, Shakespeare's greatest plays are generally considered to be his four mature tragedies, *Hamlet, Othello, King Lear* and *Macbeth*.

Tragedy

Key skills: communication – discussion

1 Consider the following brief scenario:
   While 'shinning' down a drainpipe, having stolen a video recorder, a burglar slipped and fell to his death.
   On your own, consider how 'tragic' you consider this to be. Be prepared to justify your response to others.
2 Now record how your responses change (if they do change) when you read the following information:
   a the burglar had a wife and two small children at home.
   b the burglar had recently been made redundant and wanted to buy some clothes for his children.
   c the burglar had recently been made redundant and wanted to buy some clothes for himself.

d the burglar was stealing the video back after it had originally been stolen by the occupants of the house he was burgling.

e the burglar was a child, working for adults who were making him steal.

3 Now share your responses as a group. Find areas of agreement and disagreement. Based on this, produce a group definition *in one paragraph* of tragedy.

4 Now read the following quotations which contain some other definitions of tragedy. In your groups, discuss what these quotations have to say about tragedy. To what extent are they similar to or different from the ideas you have already recorded?

5 Now focus particularly on those parts of the quotations in bold type. What are they suggesting about tragedy? To what extent do you agree with them?

'sad stories **of commonwealths and kings**' (Isidore of Seville, 6th–7th centuries AD)

'a poem written in the grand style, **which treats of shameful or wicked deeds**, and beginning in joy, ends in grief.' (John of Garland, 12th–13th centuries AD)

'the high and excellent Tragedy, that openeth the greatest wounds, and showeth forth the ulcers covered with tissue' (Sir Philip Sidney, *An Apologie for Poesy,* c. 1579)

'**that majestic sadness** which constitutes the whole pleasure of tragedy' (Jean Racine, 1688)

'In a tragedy, nothing is in doubt and everyone's destiny is known. That makes for tranquillity. There is a sort of fellow-feeling among characters in a tragedy: he who kills is as innocent as he who gets killed: it's all a matter of what part you are playing. **Tragedy is restful**; and the reason is that hope, that foul, deceitful thing, has no part in it. There isn't any hope. You're trapped. The whole sky has fallen in on you, and all you can do about it is to shout.' (Jean Anouilh, *Antigone*, 1942)

COMMENTARY   Like drama itself, tragedy is a word used a great deal in the modern press, usually to mean an event which is highly unfortunate and which has had disastrous consequences. It may well be that your definition followed these lines. However, also like the word drama, tragedy as a literary genre has a set number of specific elements which set it apart from common conceptions of the word, although related to them:

■ Tragedy is usually about one central figure, the *protagonist*, and the play charts their fall from a position of power to their ultimate shaming or death (a reversal of Fortune – *peripeteia*). Often others die with them – known as the 'multiple death convention'.

■ The protagonist, or 'tragic hero', is normally a figure of considerable importance and is often royal. Their death therefore does not just have an individual impact, but affects the whole state (for example, *Oedipus, Hamlet*).

■ The tragic hero is a person with an exceptional nature, with the ability to feel emotions in an intensified way. However, they can possess a 'flaw', a fault which would normally be insignificant, but which is revealed by the chain of events and leads directly to their downfall (for example Macbeth's ambition, or Othello's jealousy). This is known as *hamartia*.

■ The protagonist often upsets the natural order of things, whether deliberately or not. For example, Orestes does so in murdering his mother in Aeschylus' *Oresteia*. The play ends with order in some way being restored.

- Through the protagonist's death, we see a waste of human life, but we also see the nobility of the characters who died: they demonstrate human greatness.
- The important role played by fate. In Greek tragedy, the tragic hero is seen as a plaything of the gods, often fated to commit certain acts and unable to avoid them, although their character (with its fatal flaw) in some way helps to lead to their downfall. In Shakespearean tragedy, there remains a sense of divine order – 'There's some divinity that shapes our ends,/Rough hew them what we will' as Hamlet says – although generally characters have more control over their own behaviour. However, they are often misguided and act blindly (for example, Macbeth is tricked by the witches).
- The effect on the audience. The most famous theory as to the benefit of tragedy to an audience was again suggested by Aristotle, who awarded tragedy an almost therapeutic, or *cathartic,* effect. Through being exposed to horrific acts and terrible incidents, any similar emotions the audience feels are purged during the course of the play. Do you agree with this idea? What does it have to say about violence on the modern stage, or in film?

ACTIVITY 13

Key skills: communication – writing documents

1 Take a nursery rhyme or fairy story you know well and rewrite it so that it clearly follows some of the 'rules' of tragedy as outlined above. Feel free to change the story if necessary! You could try some of the following:
   The Tragedy of the Gingerbread Man
   Humpty Dumpty: A Woeful Tragedy
   The Lamentable Tale of Jack and Jill
   The Troll from 'Three Billy Goats Gruff': A Tragic Hero?

2 If you are very ambitious, write the stories as short playscripts and then perform them. The rest of the class can then determine how they fit the rules of tragedy.

3 Take one of Shakespeare's tragedies you have studied or familiarise yourself with one (you do not necessarily have to read it for this Activity – there are plenty of good film versions, for example Polanski's *Macbeth* or Kenneth Branagh's *Hamlet*). Consider to what extent your chosen tragedy fits the 'rules' of tragedy as outlined above.

A Brief History of Drama

The origins of western drama: Greek tragedy

Although there is evidence of types of ritual and performance existing in different societies for thousands of years, drama as we know it – that is, as acted to an audience and involving dialogue between characters – first evolved in Ancient Greece and reached its peak in the fifth century BC, when tragedies (meaning 'goat-song' from the Greek *tragos*, 'goat' probably because goats were sacrificed) were performed at the *Dionysia*, a dramatic festival held in Athens every April in honour of the Greek God of wine and song, Dionysus. These tragedies had a huge influence on Elizabethan drama and the plays are still performed today.

This drama probably developed from songs and rituals performed by a 'Chorus' of fifty Athenian men in honour of Dionysus. The grand job of having invented drama is given to a character called Thespis, who was apparently the first member of the Chorus to step out and then address them in the character of a god, thus creating dialogue. That is why actors even today are known as 'Thespians'. This early drama was probably fairly crude, but by the time of Aeschylus, Sophocles and Euripides, the three great Athenian dramatists, tragedy was a popular, sophisticated and well-funded enterprise, and preparations for the Dionysia began months in advance. There was even what we would call a modern day 'producer', the *choregus*, whose job was to raise funds for the plays to be performed at the Dionysia, and they even had a form of special effects, the *deus ex machina* – a crane which allowed the gods to 'fly'!

Theatre of Dionysia at Athens

Each playwright had to submit four plays: a trilogy of tragedies and then what was known as a satyr play (a satyr being half-goat, half-man), which was a hybrid of comedy and tragedy and dealt with similar themes to the three tragedies. For their subject matter, the playwrights always chose common myths which the audience would know. That being the case, the element of surprise was lost, but instead greater emphasis was placed on the dramatist's treatment of the myth. The two most famous existing trilogies are Aeschylus' *Oresteia*, telling of the myth of Orestes, and Sophocles' so-called *Theban trilogy*, telling the story of Oedipus and his daughter Antigone. The tragedies generally portray humans as being at the mercy of gods who are at best thoughtless and at worst malicious, and subject to a fate which can often be cruel. The protagonists (main characters) of these plays often find themselves in situations in which they have no control, or in impossible dilemmas which ultimately lead to their death. Perhaps the most famous example of this 'malign fate' is Sophocles' story of *Oedipus*. A summary of the story and then an extract from the play follows.

ACTIVITY 14

Key skills: communication – reading/discussion

Read the following summary of the story of *Oedipus* and then the extract from Sophocles' play. Then in groups, discuss the following.

1 Bearing in mind that the audience would already have known the myth of Oedipus, what is Sophocles' intention in prolonging the scene for as long as he does?

2 Take note of all the things Tiresias says which suggest he knows that Oedipus is the killer. What effect would this have on the audience?

3 From your understanding of the story from the summary, and your reaction to Oedipus as he appears in the extract, how much sympathy do you have for him? To what extent is he a victim and to what extent is he to blame?

The Story of Oedipus

Before Oedipus is born, his parents visit the Oracle, which predicts that he will marry his own mother and murder his father. Horrified, they bolt his ankles together (hence his name, meaning 'swollen foot') and leave him to die on a mountain-top. However, he is found by a shepherd, who pities him and gives him to a childless couple who bring him up as their own son, never telling him how they had found him. One day, Oedipus hears a joke about him 'not being his father's son' and goes to the Oracle to discover the truth. On being told the prophecy, he flees to Thebes in order to avoid it. On the way he has an argument with a man in a carriage who refuses to move to one side of the road; he strikes and kills him. When he arrives in Thebes, he discovers that the city is being terrorised by the evil monster, the Sphinx, who refuses to leave until her riddles have been answered. Oedipus saves the city by solving the Sphinx's riddle and as a reward is offered the hand of the older Queen of Thebes, Jocasta, who has recently been widowed when her husband, Laius, was attacked. Oedipus marries Jocasta and becomes King of Thebes. They have two children, but then a strange plague hits the city. Oedipus sends his kinsman Creon to the Oracle to discover the cause of the plague; and the Oracle reveals it is because Laius's killer is still in Thebes. Oedipus sends for the prophet Tiresias, determined to find out the truth. It soon becomes apparent that the man Oedipus had killed on the road was his father and his wife, the Queen, is his mother. The prophecy has come true. On discovering this, Jocasta hangs herself and Oedipus blinds himself by stabbing out his eyes with her brooch-pin.

Sophocles' play *Oedipus Tyrannos* (*King Oedipus*) focuses on the last third of the myth of Oedipus, his *anagnorisis* (a common convention in Greek tragedy, 'the revelation') in which he discovers the truth about his parents and the prophecy. The play opens with Oedipus addressing the crowd in the hope of finding out the cause of the plague. The following extract is at the point when the prophet Tiresias has been summoned to reveal the truth.

> OEDIPUS: What's this? Why so grim, so dire?
> TIRESIAS: Just send me home. You bear your burdens,
> I'll bear mine. It's better that way,
> please believe me.
> OEDIPUS: Strange response ... unlawful,
> unfriendly too to the state that bred and reared you –
> you withhold the word of god.
> TIRESIAS: I fail to see
> that your own words are so well-timed.
> I'd rather not have the same thing said of me ...
> OEDIPUS: For the love of god, don't turn away,
> not if you know something. We beg you,
> all of us on our knees.
> TIRESIAS: None of you knows –
> and I will never reveal my dreadful secrets,
> not to say your own.
> OEDIPUS: What? You know and you won't tell?
> You're bent on betraying us, destroying Thebes?
> TIRESIAS: I'd rather not cause pain for you or me.
> So why this ... useless interrogation?
> You'll get nothing from me.
> OEDIPUS: Nothing! You,
> you scum of the earth, you'd enrage a heart of stone!
> You won't talk? Nothing moves you?
> Out with it, once and for all!
> TIRESIAS: You criticize my temper ... unaware
> of the one you live with, you revile me.
> OEDIPUS: Who could restrain his anger, hearing you?
> What outrage – you spurn the city!
> TIRESIAS: What will come will come.
> Even if I shroud it all in silence.
> OEDIPUS: What will come? You're bound to tell me that.
> TIRESIAS: I will say no more. Do as you like, build your anger
> to whatever pitch you please, rage your worst –
> OEDIPUS: Oh, I'll let loose. I have such fury in me –
> now I see it all. You helped hatch the plot,
> you did the work, yes, short of killing him
> with your own hands – and given eyes I'd say
> you did the killing single-handed!
> TIRESIAS: Is that so!
> I charge you, then, submit to that decree
> you just laid down: from this day onward
> speak to no one, not these citizens, not myself.
> *You* are the curse, the corruption of the land!

(*King Oedipus*, Sophocles, trans. Robert Fagles)

COMMENTARY:
Dramatic irony and the tragic flaw

As the audience will already have been familiar with the story of Oedipus, clearly they will realise his foolishness in pushing for the truth, and will recognise the hidden meanings in Tiresias' comments, such as 'I'd rather not cause pain for you or me'. In many ways the scene could be described as excruciating, as we the audience have a greater knowledge than the character on stage and so can see the irony in his insistence on finding out the true murderer – even to the extent that he accuses Tiresias of the murder! This technique is known as *dramatic irony*, and is a very common one which can be used effectively in both tragedy and comedy. In this case the dramatic irony is so effective because of the very serious consequences we know the discovery will have for Oedipus. However, you can easily imagine the dramatic potential in a situation where the audience are let into a secret the characters themselves do not know. It is a common device in Shakespearean and Restoration comedy, as well as in modern television comedies. The modern 'sitcom', or situation comedy, often revolves around a situation in which a character's ignorance is exploited – much to the audience's delight.

ACTIVITY 15

Key skills: communication – discussion/presentation

In groups, think of two fairly simple situations involving the use of dramatic irony. One should use the dramatic irony for comic effect and one should be serious (for an example of dramatic irony in comedy, see the extract from Sheridan's *Rivals* on page 59). When you have done this, improvise a short scene based around it and present it to the class.

The Tragic Flaw – Oedipus, Aristotle and A. C. Bradley

It would clearly be unfair to suggest that Oedipus' horrific downfall is his own fault; he is a victim of a cruel Fate which was prophesied before his birth and which he attempts to avoid. In this sense he is completely blameless. However, as Aristotle said, 'Character is Destiny', and in some ways Oedipus' 'reversal of fortune' (*peripeteia*) is sealed by his own behaviour. He is impetuous and short-tempered, something which made him fight and kill his own father and which also is demonstrated in the extract where, in a fast and furious exchange (known in Greek Tragedy as *stichomythia*), he very quickly loses his temper with Tiresias and actually goads him into revealing the truth. This short fuse is something Tiresias himself recognises when he says 'You criticize my temper . . . unaware of the one you live with'.

Clearly, Oedipus is not wholly innocent. Although a victim, he plays a role in his own downfall. Aristotle again suggested (using Oedipus as his model) that a tragic character should possess some flaws in order to stir the audience's sympathy and the critic A. C. Bradley picked up on this in the early twentieth century when he identified what he called a 'tragic flaw' in each of Shakespeare's tragic characters. For Bradley, these flaws were not of minor importance – they were the elements of their characters which brought about their downfall. Modern critics have accepted that this argument is slightly forced – it is not just ambition which destroys Macbeth, after all – but it remains an influential, if over-simplistic, idea.

TERMINOLOGY BOX 2

A Tragic Vocabulary

The following terms were all applied to Greek tragedy, although they can also be used in discussion of modern drama.

Anagnorisis: A revelation, or a moment of self-discovery.

Deus ex Machina: the crane by which gods flew in as saviours at the end of a Greek play. The term is used nowadays to refer to a device at the end of a play in which characters are saved or problems are resolved.

Hamartia: a character's flaw.

Hubris: an act of arrogance, where a character oversteps the mark. Usually followed automatically by *nemesis.*

Nemesis: Goddess of retribution; also refers to someone who avenges or punishes.

Peripeteia: a reversal of Fortune.

Protagonist: (literally, first speaker): the main character in a tragedy.

Stychomythia: a technique of quickfire dialogue.

Greek and Roman Comedy

Tragedy was not the only genre of Greek drama. There was also a strong tradition of comedy split into two different eras, 'Old' and 'New', which can be broadly represented by two playwrights: Aristophanes for the 'Old' and Menander for the 'New'. Aristophanes' comedy, of which we have a number of complete plays including *The Frogs* and *The Wasps*, was topical, satirical and very, very rude. Menander is the only example we have of the so-called 'New' comedy, and his plays are only in fragments. Nevertheless, it is clear that this later comedy is very different from that of Aristophanes. It is not political, but is instead of a fairly inoffensive kind, concerning itself with situations in everyday life.

It was this 'New' comedy which acted as a model for Roman Comedy, the most popular genre in Ancient Rome. Roman drama has been generally accepted as inferior to that of the Greeks, although the main Roman comic playwrights, Plautus and Terence, based their plays on those of the Greeks. Their main importance is in their influence on English Elizabethan drama – for example, Plautus' *Menaechmi* formed the basis for Shakespeare's *Comedy of Errors*. Although we know most about comic writers, probably because of their greater popularity, the most important of all is the Roman tragedist Seneca, as it was the re-discovery of his gory interpretations of Greek myths such as *Oedipus* in the Renaissance that produced the fashion for revenge tragedy which dominated the Elizabethan and Jacobean stage.

Some plays to read from this period are:

Aeschylus, *The Oresteia* (translated by Ted Hughes)

Sophocles, *The Theban Trilogy* (c. 450–400 BC)

Aristophanes, *The Frogs* (c. 450–400 BC)

Plautus, *The Pot of Gold*

Seneca, *Thyestes*

Drama in Medieval England (1350–1550)

After the great civilisations of Greece and Rome, historians refer to a period known as The Dark Ages in which very little literature of any worth was produced, and this is also true for drama. In fact, some performances of Roman writers like Terence continued, but the main source of any new dramatic forms came from the Christian Church. Just as Greek tragedy came from prayers to Dionysus, drama of the Middle Ages evolved from performances of famous Biblical stories such as those of Noah, Herod and Christ. They were first performed by priests only, in Latin and in churches, but then – in a huge breakthrough in the history of English drama – the plays moved out of the churches and began to be performed by everyday people, in English as it was spoken at the time. Non-religious aspects were added – most particularly in comedy – and a form of theatre, the 'Mystery Plays', appeared.

The Mystery Plays, such as those in York and Chester, were small scenes performed in cycles, either in one place rather like a modern 'in-the-round' stage, or in travelling 'pageants' in which the scenes were performed on a small cart that travelled around repeating the scenes in its cycle.

Tradesmen from different guilds (for example, carpenters or fishmongers) were given the responsibility for creating the set for the particular story they were retelling, often with an appropriate link (the carpenters might build Noah's Ark, for instance).

Again like Greek Tragedy, although Medieval Drama clearly had religious roots and the subject matter remained religious, the dramatic forms very quickly moved from prayer to performance. Stock, comic characters appeared who bore little relation to their Biblical counterparts and could almost have been blasphemous. Noah very quickly became the hen-pecked husband of his nagging wife; Herod became famous for his ranting and shouting (talking of an actor, Hamlet says he 'out-Herods Herod'). Even Satan himself was given comic treatment in some Mystery Plays, and a host of smaller comic parts were created for the audiences' entertainment, such as the dim-witted shepherds in the nativity plays (in many ways, school nativity plays continue the Mystery Play tradition). Along with added *dramatic* (as opposed to purely *religious*) characters, came *theatrical* aspects of performance, which were very advanced. The Mystery Plays kept the church convention of using one side of the stage to represent heaven and one side to represent hell and, like the Greek *deus ex machina*, the Mystery Plays had cranes which allowed God and his angels to fly in the heavens on one side, while the other side presented a realistic interpretation of Hell's Mouth, complete with fire and smoke. Other special effects, such as severed limbs, were also used!

A slightly later form of drama, with a religious basis but which did not simply retell Biblical stories, was the Morality Play. These were plays which, as their name suggests, taught their audiences important morals about Christian living, through allegorical stories about abstract vices, such as Gluttony, Lust and Sloth, and their constant war on Christian virtues such as Patience and Chastity. These personified Vices and Virtues represented the struggle of humans to lead a good Christian life and showed the trials and tribulations of a soul on the way to Heaven, in plays such as *The Castle of Perseverance* (1425) and in the most famous morality play *Everyman* (1500). In themselves, these plays are not necessarily great examples of dramatic literature; however, they paved the way for what could be described as England's greatest dramatic period – the Renaissance. (For an exploration of the way in which Medieval Drama influenced Renaissance Drama, look at the discussion of the contexts of *Doctor Faustus* in Chapter 4.)

ACTIVITY 16

Key skills: communication: reading/making a presentation

In groups, take the following extract from *Noah's Flood*, and prepare a performance of it. Each group should then show their performance. As a class, discuss the piece's effectiveness. How well crafted is it? Does it have any noticeable dramatic devices? How does the extract deal with time?

Noah's Flood, from The Chester Pageant

NOAH: Ah, Lord, I thanke thee lowd and still,
    That to me art in such will,
    And spares me and my house to spill,
    As now I *soothlie* fynde.   *soothlie*: truly
    Thy bydding, Lord, I shall fulfil,
    And never more thee greeve ne *grill*,   *grill*: worry
    That suche grace has sent me till
    Among all mankinde.
    Have done, yow men and women all!
    Helpe for ought that may befall,
    To worke this shipp, chamber and hall,
    As God hath bydden us doe.
SHEM: Father, I am all ready *bowne*:   *bowne*: prepared
    Anne axe I have, by my crown,
    As sharpe as any in all this town,
    For to goe ther-to.
HAM: I have a hatchet wonder-kene
    To byte well, as may be seene;
    A better *grownden*, as I *wene*,   *grownden*: sharper one
    Is not in all this towne.   *wene*: think
JAPHETH: And I can well make a pyn,
    And with this hammer knocke yt in;
    Goe and worche without more *dynne*,   *dynne*: noise
    And I am ready bowne.

NOAH'S WIFE: And we shall bring tymber to,
 For wee mun nothing els doe;
 Women be weake to underfoe
 Any great *travayle*.   *travayle*: work
SHEM'S WIFE: Here is a good hackstock;
 On this yow may hew and knock;
 Shall none be idle in this flocke,
 Ne now may no man fail.
HAM'S WIFE: And I will go to gather sliche,
 The ship for to cleane and piche;
 Anoynted it must be every stich,
 Board, tree and pyn.
JAPHETH'S WIFE: And I will gather chippes here
 To make a fire for yow *in feere*,   *in feere*: all together
 And for to *dight* your dynner,   *dight*: cook
 Against yow come in.
 (They then make different signs, as if working
 with different tools.)
NOAH: Now in the name of God I will begin
 To make the shippe that we shall in,
 That we be ready for to swym
 At the cominge of the flood.
 These bordes I joyne here together,
 To keep us safe from the wedder,
 That we may rowe both hither and thider,
 And safe be from this floode.
 Of this tree will I make the mast,
 Tyde with gables that will last,
 With a sayle-yarde for each blast,
 And each thinge in ther kinde,
 With topcastle and bewsprytt,
 With coardes and ropes I hold all meete
 To sayle forth at the next *weete*;   *weete*: downpour
 This ship is at an ende.

Some plays to read in this period are:

The York and Chester Mystery Cycles (14th century)

Everyman (c. 1500–1510)

Drama in the Renaissance (1550–1642)

The Renaissance (or 'Rebirth') in England was part of a wider cultural change which began in Italy in the early sixteenth century, in which a 'rediscovery' of the classics created a revolution in the arts, one of which was the theatre. In England, this resulted in a move away from the religious and allegorical plays of the Middle Ages, to the works of Shakespeare and Ben Jonson – and in a very short period of time.

The first real play of the Renaissance was *Gorboduc*, a tragedy written by Thomas Norton and Thomas Sackville in 1562, which owed a considerable amount to the plays of the Roman dramatist Seneca. Seneca's plays had recently been translated from the original Latin and their popularity created a blueprint for many of the tragedies produced on the Elizabethan and Jacobean stage, known as *revenge tragedies*. These were a specific sub-genre of tragedy which usually began with a ghost appearing to reveal that it had been foully murdered and asking a character to revenge its death. The chain of events which followed invariably led to everyone's death – the 'multiple death convention'. Like those of Seneca, the plays were often very gruesome, playing on the audience's fascination with blood and gore, and it was Seneca who also provided a model for the five acts in which most tragedies took place. All the great playwrights of the Renaissance produced plays in this popular genre: Shakespeare's *Titus Andronicus* and *Hamlet* and Christopher Marlowe's *Jew of Malta* are good examples, and there were countless other, lesser playwrights such as Thomas Kyd, John Ford and Cyril Tourneur who produced a great number. Perhaps the playwright best remembered solely for his bloodthirsty tragedies is John Webster (for an extract from *The Duchess of Malfi*, see page 68). Although the Renaissance is most famous for its bloody tragedies, comedy also continued on the Elizabethan stage. *Ralph Roister Doister*, the first Elizabethan comedy, appeared in the decade before *Gorboduc*. Shakespeare wrote as many comedies as tragedies and Ben Jonson had more success in his comedies than his tragedies in the first half of the seventeenth century.

Although theatrically popular and successful, the plays in the Elizabethan age were also profoundly interested in the moral and philosophical issues of their age. The tragedies questioned the very nature of humanity and considered such topics as our moral nature, the role of fate and the existence of evil. These issues were presented in plays with energy and vitality, and the comedies too were fresh, vibrant and (most importantly) very funny. For many, the Elizabethan age represents a Golden Age in English Literature.

The Elizabethan Theatre

The first main Elizabethan theatre was built by the actor and carpenter James Burbage in 1576. It was called simply The Theatre, from the Greek 'place to see', and was originally set outside London, in Finsbury Fields, as acting was not considered to be a wholesome activity and would not be tolerated within the city boundaries. The fact that 21 years later, when its lease ran out, it uprooted and moved to the South Bank to become The Globe, where most of Shakespeare's plays were performed, demonstrates the huge popular success of the theatre, and others sprang up quickly, such as The Rose and The Swan.

Our evidence for the appearance of an Elizabethan theatre is based largely on a drawing of The Swan made by a Dutch visitor, Johannes de Witt. It reveals that there were two levels for the audiences; the more expensive galleries for those who could afford them, and an open space in front of the stage with room for standing viewers – the famous 'groundlings'. The stage, which was raised probably between four to six feet, thrust out into this audience, and people could gather round tightly and take a close-up view of the action. The theatre was also open air and was usually shaped to be octagonal, or roughly round – Shakespeare famously described The Globe as 'this wooden O' in *Henry V.* Performances would take place in daylight, often in poor weather conditions and with a lively, sometimes rowdy audience. The experience of a theatre-goer in Elizabethan times would have been very different to today; in many ways, it holds more in common with a football match!

The Swan Theatre by Johannes de Witt

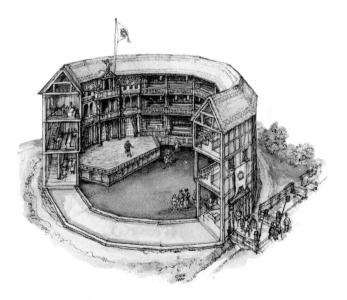

The Rose Theatre by C. Walter Hodges

**Key skills: communication –
research/making a presentation**

Based on the information you have been given
on Elizabethan theatre, work in pairs to
produce a plan of a web-page explaining the
major differences between the Elizabethan and
modern theatre which should be taken into
account when studying an Elizabethan play.

Three Elizabethan Playwrights: Marlowe, Shakespeare and Jonson

The first playwright to produce plays of any real quality on the Elizabethan
stage was **Christopher Marlowe** (for his biography, see page 88), whose
tragedies *Tamburlaine I and II, Doctor Faustus, The Jew of Malta, Edward
II* and *Dido, Queen of Carthage* were a roaring success. Although Marlowe's
plays still owed something to earlier drama, his inestimable contribution to
English drama was to create characters with a degree of what we call
psychological realism – that is, with the appearance of being real individuals
with a mind and thoughts of their own, rather than simply representing
abstract concepts, as in the earlier Morality Plays. Marlowe in his time was
as popular as the up-and-coming William Shakespeare, and may well have
gone on to produce even greater plays, were it not for an untimely death in
mysterious circumstances in a pub-brawl.

William Shakespeare was an actor and poet from Stratford who had turned
his hand to play writing. Unlike other writers of his time, he didn't attend
university and was once described as possessing 'little Latin and less Greek',
although in his book *The Genius of Shakespeare* Jonathan Bate suggests this
wasn't necessarily the case. Even so, Shakespeare was something of an
'outsider', but had the knack of producing plays which were very successful
and gave the audience exactly what they wanted, from the blood and guts of
Titus Andronicus to the ribald comedies he produced, such as *Love's Labours
Lost*. Shakespeare was writing from the early 1590s, but it was under the
monarch King James I that his best plays were produced, the famous mature
tragedies, which have since become the keystones of English literature –
King Lear, Hamlet, Macbeth and *Othello*. (For a more detailed look at
Shakespeare, see the chapter in *Living Literature*).

Whereas the plays of Shakespeare were considered earthy and home-grown,
those of **Ben Jonson** were lofty, sophisticated and full of classical
references. Like Marlowe, Jonson was a lively character and was often in
trouble with the authorities, once for killing a man in a duel! His tragedies
were quickly forgotten, but his satirical comedies such as *Volpone* and *The
Alchemist* remain popular today. Jonson was greatly respected in his life-
time, even more respected than Shakespeare, and was made the first official
Poet Laureate.

The Civil War and the end of Renaissance Theatre

After the flowering that produced such writers as Marlowe, Shakespeare
and Jonson, the quality of the drama produced on the English stage waned
fairly quickly. With odd exceptions, such as John Webster, the plays that
were being performed were weaker, and so were the actors who acted them.
The theatres had already been closed once late in the sixteenth century

because of the plague, but in their heyday had survived to re-open. But when the **civil war** broke out in 1642, with the monarchy being deposed by a largely **Puritan** force led by **Oliver Cromwell**, English drama was a diseased animal, and was also considered to be an immoral one at that, representing the indulgent entertainment of a Royalist age. The theatres were closed by the Puritans and acting was forbidden. Some theatre continued secretly but, to all intents and purposes, drama was temporarily at a standstill. When it was to reappear in 1660, it had undergone a significant change.

ACTIVITY 18

Key skills: information technology: sources/select information

Individually, use the Internet to research the English Civil War, focusing particularly on those words in bold in the previous section.

ACTIVITY 19

Key skills: communication – reading/discussion

The following extract is from near the end of the most famous revenge tragedy, *Hamlet*. Read it in groups, and then discuss the following questions.

- Make sure you fully understand the order of events as they occur in the extract. Who dies, when, and why?

- Comment on the ways in which the scene will have an impact on the audience.
- What do you make of the 'multiple death convention' as it appears here? Does it work dramatically? What does our response to it tell us about the use of conventions in the theatre?

Hamlet, by William Shakespeare (1600)

Hamlet is about to duel with Laertes, whose sword has secretly been tipped with poison, the work of both Laertes and King Claudius, who wants him dead and who has also poisoned a cup of wine as an extra precaution.

HAMLET: Come on, sir.
LAERTES: Come, my lord. *(They play)*
HAMLET: One.
LAERTES: No.
HAMLET: Judgment.
OSRIC: A hit, a very palpable hit.
LAERTES: Well, again.
KING: Stay, give me drink. Hamlet, this pearl is thine.
Here's to thy health. *(Drums; trumpets; and shot goes off)*
Give him the cup.
HAMLET: I'll play this bout first. Set it by awhile.
Come. *(They play again)*
Another hit. What say you?
LAERTES: I do confess't.
KING: Our son shall win.
QUEEN: He's fat and scant of breath.
Here, Hamlet, take my napkin, rub thy brows.
The Queen carouses to thy fortune, Hamlet.
HAMLET: Good madam.

KING: Gertrude, do not drink.
QUEEN: I will, my lord, I pray you pardon me.
(She drinks and offers the cup to Hamlet)
KING: *(aside)* It is the poison'd cup. It is too late.
HAMLET: I dare not drink yet, madam – by and by.
QUEEN: Come, let me wipe thy face.
LAERTES: My lord, I'll hit him now.
KING: I do not think't.
LAERTES: *(aside)* And yet it is almost against my conscience.
HAMLET: Come for the third, Laertes. You do but dally.
I pray you pass with your best violence.
I am afeard you make a wanton of me.
LAERTES: Say you so? Come on. *(They play)*
OSRIC: Nothing neither way.
LAERTES: Have at you now. *(Laertes wounds Hamlet; then, in scuffling, they change rapiers.)*
KING: Part them; they are incens'd.
HAMLET: Nay, come again. *(He wounds Laertes. The Queen falls.)*
OSRIC: Look to the Queen there, ho!
HORATIO: They bleed on both sides. How is it, my lord?
OSRIC: How is't, Laertes?
LAERTES: Why, as a woodcock to mine own springe, Osric.
I am justly killed with mine own treachery.
HAMLET: How does the Queen?
KING: She swoons to see them bleed.
QUEEN: No, no, the drink, the drink! O my dear Hamlet!
The drink, the drink! I am poison'd.   *Dies.*
HAMLET: O villainy! Ho! Let the door be lock'd.
Treachery! Seek it out!   *Exit Osric.*
LAERTES: It is here, Hamlet. Hamlet, thou art slain.
No medicine in the world can do thee good;
In thee there is not half an hour's life.
The treacherous instrument is in thy hand,
Unbated and envenomed. The foul practice
Hath turn'd itself on me. Lo, here I lie,
Never to rise again. Thy mother's poisoned.
I can no more. The King – the King's to blame.
HAMLET: The point envenomed, too? Then, venom, do thy work.

                                                                  Wounds the king.

ALL: Treason! Treason!
KING: O yet defend me friends. I am but hurt.
HAMLET: Here, thou incestuous, murd'rous, damned Dane,
Drink off this potion. Is thy union here?
Follow my mother.   *King dies.*
LAERTES: He is justly served.
It is a poison temper'd by himself.
Exchange forgiveness with me, noble Hamlet.
Mine and thy father's death come not upon thee,
Nor thine on me.   *Dies.*

                                                      Hamlet, Act V sc. 2

Some texts worth reading from this period are:

Thomas Kyd, *The Spanish Tragedy* (1587)

Christopher Marlowe, *Doctor Faustus* (1592)

William Shakespeare, *Much Ado about Nothing* (1598), *Hamlet* (1600), *Henry V* (1598), *Macbeth* (1605)

Ben Jonson, *Volpone* (1606), *The Alchemist* (1610)

John Webster, *The Duchess of Malfi* (1614)

Thomas Middleton, *The Changeling* (1622)

Restoration Drama (1660–1770): Women take the stage

When Charles II returned from exile and was restored to the throne in 1660 (hence 'Restoration'), theatre was re-established but with many changes. Courtly tastes were now decidedly 'continental' and when the theatres were refurbished they followed the new continental style, abandoning the thrust stages of the Elizabethans and instead using the 'proscenium arches' that are still in evidence today. Set and costume became very elaborate and, following continental custom, for the first time women were allowed to take the stage (previously, female parts had been played by men, with small boys playing young women and older men playing such comic roles as the Nurse in *Romeo and Juliet*). It is also in this period that the first female professional playwright, Aphra Behn, appears although she was not the only female dramatist of the Renaissance – others, such as the mysterious 'Ariadne' or Susanna Centlivre, produced plays which were as popular as those produced by men, if not at times more so. (It is an interesting aspect of English Literature that these playwrights have been neglected, something feminist criticism has attempted to redress.)

Tastes had also changed and the works of writers like Shakespeare and Jonson were considered unrefined and too barbarous for performance – or at least, if they were performed, it was in new adaptations by writers such as Dryden or Tate which removed any of the more offensive elements. Tate, for example, rewrote *King Lear* to give it a happy ending! In fact, this was an age in which tragedy was much neglected – its seriousness, its morality and above all its vulgarity didn't accord with an age in which manners and etiquette were the order of the day.

Initially, new audiences had to make do with adapted versions of older plays, but soon a new kind of drama appeared which was absolutely of its time – the comedies of manners which we call Restoration Comedy. These comedies focused around the intrigues and love-affairs of so-called gentlemen and ladies, gaining much of their comedy from the deceit and deception of characters obsessed with worldly wealth and appearance. These characters were often stock 'types', such as the young man seeking wealth by marrying the old, lusty widow, and the comedy was often on a very superficial level. Much Restoration drama could be said to be more successful as theatre than as literature (an important distinction, as Chapter 1 makes clear). At its best, however, it worked very well as both, being very funny and also providing an at times scathing commentary of the moral decadence of the society it presented, for example in Congreve's *The Way of the World.*

ACTIVITY 20

Key skills: communication – reading/discussion

Read the following example from a Restoration Comedy and, in groups, discuss to what extent

it fits the conventions described above. Where does the humour lie? What use is made of stage conventions?

(Sir George Airy is in love with Miranda, an heiress worth thirty thousand pounds who is also secretly in love with him. However, Miranda is under the guardianship of Sir Francis Gripe, an old miser who wants to marry Miranda himself so he can claim her inheritance. In this extract, Sir George has paid Sir Francis one hundred pounds for an hour with Miranda to persuade her of his love; Miranda has been forbidden to speak to him.)

SIR GEORGE: Madam, whether you'll excuse or blame my love, the author of this rash proceeding depends upon your pleasure, as also the life of your admirer! Your sparkling eyes speak a heart susceptible of love; your vivacity a soul too delicate to admit the embraces of decayed mortality.

MIRANDA: *(aside)* Oh! That I durst speak –

SIR GEORGE: Shake off this tyrant guardian's yoke, assume yourself, and dash his bold aspiring hopes; the deity of his desires, avarice; a heretic in love, and ought to be banished by the Queen of Beauty. See, madam, a faithful servant kneels and begs to be admitted in the number of your slaves.

(Miranda gives him her hand to raise him.)

SIR FRANCIS: I wish I could hear what he says now *(running up)* Hold, hold, hold, no palming, that's contrary to articles –

SIR GEORGE: 'Sdeath, sir keep your distance, or I'll write another article in your guts. *(Lays his hand to his sword)*

SIR FRANCIS: *(going back)* A bloody minded fellow – !

SIR GEORGE: Not answer me! Perhaps she thinks my address too grave: I'll be more free – can you be so unconscionable, madam, to let me say all these fine things to you without one single compliment in return? View me well, am I not a proper handsome fellow, ha? Can you prefer that old, dry, withered sapless log of sixty-five, to the vigorous, gay, sprightly love of twenty-four? With snoring only he'll wake thee, but I with ravishing delight would make thy senses dance in consort with the joyful minutes. – Ha! Not yet? Sure she is dumb? – Thus would I steal and touch thy beauteous hand, *(takes hold of her hand)*, till by degrees, I reached thy snowy breasts, then ravish kisses thus. *(Embraces her in the ecstasy)*

MIRANDA: *(struggles and flings from him) (aside)* Oh heavens, I shall not be able to contain myself.

SIR FRANCIS: *(running up with his watch in his hand)* Sure she did not speak to him – there's three-quarters of an hour gone, Sir George – adod, I don't like these close conferences –

SIR GEORGE: More interruptions – you will have it, sir. *(Lays his hand to his sword)*

SIR FRANCIS: *(aside, going back)* No, no, you shan't have her neither.

The Busybody, Susanna Centlivre (1709)

Key skills: communication – writing documents

In groups, produce a *pastiche* of a Restoration drama scene. Try to make it as mannered as possible! Try to include references to:

i an inheritance
ii a secret desire
iii a duel.

Some plays to read from this period are:

Aphra Behn, *The Rover* (1677)

John Dryden, *All for Love* (1677)

William Wycherley, *The Country Wife* (1675)

William Congreve, *The Way of the World* (1700)

Susanna Centlivre, *The Busybody* (1709)

The late eighteenth and early nineteenth century: drama in decline

It could be said that the quality of drama is only ever a reflection of the quality of its audience: it plays to audiences and needs audiences to survive. As a result, it will usually give audiences exactly what they want and in the case of Restoration drama, as the audiences' expectations became less sophisticated, so did the drama. With notable exceptions, such as Richard Sheridan and Oliver Goldsmith writing in the second half of the eighteenth century, this led to a great decline in the quality of drama in England which, it could be argued, continued through into the nineteenth century, with audiences being content with theatrical, rather than dramatic, quality. Sets became ever more elaborate and special effects became extreme. All of these aspects drew attention away from the most important thing – the drama itself – and the plots and characters became mere excuses for theatrical extravaganzas.

The plays themselves became variations on a stock theme; the sub-genre *melodrama* gained huge popularity, but the plays were rarely original, used stock characters and rarely had anything of importance to say. It is fair to say that *drama as literature* had been in decline for almost two hundred years, even though *theatre* had flourished as popular entertainment. When it finally was reinvented in a serious, literary manner – that is, as works of art – it was not in Britain (after all, why should it have been?) but in Norway and Russia.

Naturalism – Ibsen and Chekhov

The flourishing of *theatrical* aspects had meant a shift in the relative importance of the playwright in the dramatic process. Great actors, such as

Edmund Kean playing Othello, or wonderful special effects, had taken priority over the words of the script and therefore the very meaning of the play. However, the sudden emergence of the playwrights Henrik Ibsen, from Norway, and Anton Chekhov, from Russia, in the second half of the nineteenth century demonstrated that theatre could have something very important to say. Both playwrights were concerned with current social problems and dealt with them head-on in powerful, often controversial, and always thought-provoking plays: Ibsen in *A Doll's House, Ghosts, Hedda Gabler* and *The Wild Duck*, and Chekhov in *The Cherry Orchard, The Seagull* and *Uncle Vanya*. Theatre for them was not a mindless form of entertainment, but a forum for the expression of ideas with a direct relevance to people's lives. Because of this, the plays were *naturalistic*, written to be performed in a way suggesting real people talking in everyday situations. This meant that the language was no longer poetic or declamatory, as all drama had been, but was instead quiet and natural, something which drew attention away from stage performances and refocused the audience's attention on what was being said. Despite initial resistance to their ideas (see Chapter 5 for an account of this in relation to Ibsen's *A Doll's House*), they gradually became very influential and writers such as George Bernard Shaw in England became so-called 'Ibsenites,' writing about current social problems and employing the techniques of naturalism, or 'dramatic realism' as Shaw described it. It is this kind of drama, presenting us with a 'facsimile' of real life, using real props and having characters create the illusion of real thought and existence, that has become generally accepted as the mainstream of drama today, helped along by the almost absolute realism of television and film.

Of course, plays do not need to be *didactic* (teaching a lesson) or political to have a literary value; and the importance of naturalism was soon questioned by writers such as Brecht (see Chapter 5). The important step was for drama to become an *intellectual activity* again. Although one strand of theatre continued the tradition for light entertainment from the previous century, in other strands, the theatre now became the place for ideas. Encouraged by the new theories about language and representation, new plays became distinctly literary again – that is, crafted pieces of art which had a purpose beyond pure entertainment and in which the language was carefully and consciously constructed for effect. As Ibsen had done in rejecting poetry for more naturalistic expression, writers began to question forms of representation on stage, often from philosophical or linguistic angles, often forming (or, more often perhaps, being pigeon-holed into) groups of dramatists following specific theories as to the nature of drama. A brief survey of some of the major movements follows.

Expressionism

As is often the case (we have already seen one example – the Renaissance), artistic movements are not confined to one particular area of the arts. You are probably more likely to have heard of expressionism in relation to art, as a style of painting in which the artist aimed to convey his or her subjective emotions about their subject, rather than attempting to accurately portray the 'real world'. In drama, expressionism was a reaction against the realistic, naturalistic conventions of theatre as presenting things as they really were. Instead, it presented reality as biased by the emotions and memories of characters. As is often the case with literary movements, expressionism began with the plays of Strindberg almost as soon as naturalism was established, but it reached its peak in the twentieth century with writers such as Eugene O'Neill and Tennessee Williams, who said

When a play employs unconventional techniques, it is not, or certainly shouldn't be, trying to escape its responsibility of dealing with reality, or interpreting experience, but is actually or should be attempting to find a close approach, a more penetrating and vivid expression of things as they are.

(For an example of expressionism, look at the opening of Williams's *The Glass Menagerie* in the next chapter).

Theatre of the Absurd

Just as the English stage was greatly influenced by European drama through the work of Ibsen and Chekhov in the late nineteenth century, European theatre again exerted its influence with two surreal forms of drama in the twentieth. The Theatre of the Absurd derived from Paris, based largely on existentialist philosophy which focused on the purposelessness and illogicality of life, presenting humanity as an alienated species unable to communicate with others through language. If this sounds depressing, it is ironic that the main means through which these plays worked was through *farce* and *comedy*, although the term *tragicomedy* is more appropriate, as the comedy tends to be painfully grotesque, a means of reflecting on the essentially tragic nature of human existence. As Nell says in *Endgame*, one of the most famous Absurdist plays by the Irish writer Samuel Beckett (who wrote his earlier work in French), 'Nothing is funnier than unhappiness, I grant you that.'(For an extract from *Endgame*, see Chapter 5). Do you agree with Nell's theory about the relationship between comedy and tragedy?

ACTIVITY 22

Key skills: communication: making a presentation

Take the famous 'comic' scenario of someone walking down a street and slipping on a banana skin. What would it take for this to become, if not tragic, then at least slightly disturbing or *grotesque*? Write a short scene based around this idea which demonstrates the way in which comedy can have serious, or thought-provoking, effects.

ACTIVITY 23

Key skills: communication: reading/discussion

The following extract is taken from Beckett's first and most famous play, *Waiting for Godot*, originally written in French as *En Attendant Godot*. In it, two tramps, Estragon and Vladimir, wait to meet a character, Godot, who never actually turns up. While waiting, they pass the time through conversation.

1 In pairs, read the scene through two or three times. Try to emphasise the comic, clownish elements of the dialogue.
2 Now read the extract again, this time placing emphasis on its more serious aspects. In what

ways could the piece be said to present a pessimistic view of life (if you know something about *existentialism* it will help you here)? What does it have to say about the role of language and communication? What is the significance of the constant pauses?

VLADIMIR: You must have had a vision.
ESTRAGON: *(Turning his head)* What?
VLADIMIR: *(Louder)* You must have had a vision!
ESTRAGON: No need to shout!
(They resume their watch. Silence.)
VLADIMIR:
ESTRAGON: *(Turning simultaneously)* Do you –
VLADIMIR: Oh, pardon!
ESTRAGON: Carry on.
VLADIMIR: No, no, after you.
ESTRAGON: No no, you first.
VLADIMIR: I interrupted you.
ESTRAGON: On the contrary.
(They glare at each other angrily.)
VLADIMIR: Ceremonious ape!
ESTRAGON: Punctilious pig!
VLADIMIR: Finish your phrase, I tell you!
ESTRAGON: Finish your own!
(Silence. They draw closer. Halt.)
VLADIMIR: That's the idea, let's abuse each other.
(They turn, move apart, turn again and face each other.)
VLADIMIR: Moron!
ESTRAGON: Vermin!
VLADIMIR: Abortion!
ESTRAGON: Morpion!
VLADIMIR: Sewer-rat!
ESTRAGON: Curate!
VLADIMIR: Cretin!
ESTRAGON: *(with finality)* Critic!
VLADIMIR: Oh!
(He wilts, vanquished, and turns away.)
ESTRAGON: Now let's make it up.
VLADIMIR: Gogo!
ESTRAGON: Didi!
VLADIMIR: Your hand!
ESTRAGON: Take it!
VLADIMIR: Come to my arms!
ESTRAGON: Your arms?
VLADIMIR: My breast!
ESTRAGON: Off we go!
(They embrace. They separate. Silence.)
VLADIMIR: How time flies when one has fun!
(Silence.)

Waiting for Godot, Samuel Beckett (1956)

The New British Dramatists (1956–)

After the influence of Ibsen and Chekhov, there were two clear strands of drama in the twentieth century: one strand experimental, relating to literary and cultural theories and reacting against naturalism; and one strand which continued the tradition of naturalism (this is the kind of drama which has been accepted as the norm by the general public, assisted by the absolute realism of much film and television). Much of the best experimental drama produced in the earlier part of the century came from Europe, with English drama remaining naturalistic and relatively unadventurous. The so-called 'drawing room' drama dominated the English stage, as written by such dramatists as Noel Coward and Terence Rattigan, producing slick, social comedies and dramas based around the lives of generally prosperous, decent, clean-living English 'gentlemen' and 'ladies'. Although demonstrating considerable subtlety and stagecraft, these plays generally presented a cosy, middle to upper-class view of life which was a far cry from the extreme philosophy of the Theatre of the Absurd.

However, in 1956 a play was produced which was very different from these socially complacent dramas – John Osborne's *Look Back in Anger*. This was a play about anger, youth and disillusionment with the kind of values upheld in the plays of a figure like Rattigan. It was also a play about social class. Its main, dominating character, Jimmy Porter, was a university-educated member of the working-class, and one of the aspects the play explores is the sense of cultural dislocation he feels because of this. The play (for an extract, see page 111) was youthful, energetic and loosely structured, a far cry from the 'well-made plays' which had dominated the English stage. In this sense, it was as rebellious as the rock'n'roll music that was causing such a stir – Osborne was the first of a group of writers given the title 'the angry generation.'

For the first time (it seemed), youthful ideas and opinions could be seen on the stage and, for the first time, the working-class could be portrayed seriously as the subject of a play. The best example of this comes from Northern, working-class writer Shelagh Delaney, who wrote her most famous play, *A Taste of Honey*, at the age of eighteen, famously having seen a Terence Rattigan play and deciding she could do better. She felt that Rattigan 'depicts safe, sheltered, cultured lives in charmed surroundings – not life as the majority of people know it ... I had strong ideas about what I wanted to see in the theatre. We used to object to plays where factory workers come cap in hand and call the boss 'Sir'.'

Osborne and Delaney were the first of a number of writers to depict the working class sympathetically on the stage, producing another sub-genre, that of *kitchen-sink drama*, so-called because of its gritty realism. Perhaps the most famous example of this is Arnold Wesker's Trilogy *Chicken Soup with Barley*, *Roots*, and *I'm Talking about Jerusalem*. In a note to Actors and Producers, Wesker wrote:

My people are not caricatures. They are real (though fictional), and if they are to be portayed as caricatures the point of all these plays will be lost. The picture I have drawn is a harsh one, yet my tone is not one of disgust – nor should it be in the presentation of the plays.

This 'new' drama also triggered the so-called 'New Wave' of British dramatists: writers who were young, experimental and restored some of the excitement to British Theatre. These are writers such as Harold Pinter, Tom Stoppard, Edward Bond and David Edgar.

ACTIVITY 24

Key skills: communication – reading/discussion

Read the following extract from Delaney's *A Taste of Honey*. In groups, consider the following questions:

1 Arnold Wesker wrote, 'The picture I have drawn is a harsh one.' Should drama depict the 'gritty realities' of life, or should it present us with an escape from them?

2 Does drama have a social role to play, or is it purely for entertainment?

3 How different is this extract from, say, *Coronation Street*?

The stage represents a comfortless flat in Manchester and the street outside. Jazz music. Enter Helen, a semi-whore, and her daughter, Jo. They are loaded with baggage.

HELEN: Well! This is the place.

JO: And I don't like it.

HELEN: When I find somewhere for us to live I have to consider something far more important than your feelings ... the rent. It's all I can afford.

JO: You can afford something better than this old ruin.

HELEN: When you start earning you can start moaning.

JO: Can't be soon enough for me. I'm cold and my shoes let in water ... what a place ... and we're supposed to be living off her immoral earnings.

HELEN: I'm careful. Anyway, what's wrong with this place? Everything's falling apart, it's true, and we've no heating – but there's a lovely view of the gasworks, we share a bathroom with the community and this wallpaper's contemporary. What more do you want? Anyway it'll do for us. Pass me a glass, Jo.

JO: Where are they?

HELEN: I don't know.

JO: You packed 'em. She'd lose her head if it was loose.

HELEN: Here they are. I put 'em in my bag for safety. Pass me that bottle – it's in the carrier.

JO: Why should I run around after you? *(Takes whisky bottle from bag.)*

HELEN: Children owe their parents these little attentions.

JO: I don't owe you a thing.

HELEN: Except respect, and I don't seem to get any of that.

JO: Drink, drink, drink, that's all you're fit for. You make me sick.

HELEN: Others pray for their daily bread, I pray for ...

JO: Is that the bedroom?

HELEN: It is. Your health, Jo.

JO: We're sharing a bed again, I see.

HELEN: Of course, you know I can't bear to be parted from you.

JO: What I wouldn't give for a place of my own! God! It's freezing! Isn't there any sort of fire anywhere, Helen?

HELEN: Yes, there's a gas-propelled thing somewhere.

JO: Where?

HELEN: Where? What were you given eyes for? Do you want me to carry you about? Don't stand there shivering; have some of this if you're so cold.

JO: You know I don't like it.

A Taste of Honey, Shelagh Delaney (1958)

Some plays worth reading from this period are:

John Osborne, *Look Back in Anger* (1956)

Shelagh Delaney, *A Taste of Honey* (1958)

Arnold Wesker, *Roots* (1959)

Harold Pinter, *The Caretaker* (1960)

Edward Bond, *Saved* (1965)

Tom Stoppard, *The Real Inspector Hound* (1968)

Caryl Churchill, *Lights Shining in Buckinghamshire* (1976)

ACTIVITY 25

Key skills: communication – different documents

Create a poster or web-page with a time-line showing the history of English drama from 1350 to the present day. Include significant dates and names of important playwrights, if possible with pictures.

Chapter review

In this chapter, you have explored a number of different periods of drama, considering such aspects as genre, literary movements and staging.

3 Skills in Approaching Drama

This chapter looks at the craft of the playwright. You will look at some elements of technique in drama texts, such as dialogue, characterisation and stagecraft.

Assessment Objective 3 states that you must **show detailed understanding of the ways in which writers' choices of form, structure and language shape meanings.** What this means is that you have to respond to works of literature as deliberately crafted pieces of art, in which the writer employs a number of strategies and techniques with skill in order to produce a specific effect.

We saw in Chapter 1 that the dramatic form is what we can call a *working document* – in other words, it only reaches 'completion' in a performance. We also considered some of the issues and constraints involved in drama both as a literary form and as a public performance. Of course, although much of a script's appeal has to be realised in performance, if it is to be a dramatic rather than a merely theatrical success, the performance depends absolutely on the script. It is the playwright who creates the characters of the play, where they exist and what they say. The playwright's skill in using the conventions and possibilities offered by the theatre will determine the audience's response.

In this chapter you will consider some of the ways in which playwrights create specific effects on stage. We will focus on:

- Language in the plays – monologue and dialogue
- Plot structure
- Comedy
- Characterisation
- Stagecraft.

Drama – an illusion of reality

As you discovered in the previous chapter, the main tradition in drama (although not the only one, as we will see in Chapter 5) since the late nineteenth century has been *naturalistic:* that is, for playwrights to attempt to create an illusion of reality on the stage known as *verisimilitude.* We are made to feel (and often want to feel) that the characters on stage in front of us are real people; that they have thoughts, emotions, and motives; that they have a past and a future, as well as the present we see them in. The critic A. C. Bradley, writing very early in the twentieth century, is famous for the way he discussed Shakespeare's tragic characters as if they were real people, mulling over such questions as whether Lady Macbeth had any children; and if so, how many.

Of course, unless the play we are watching is based on a real event, this is a nonsense. What we are watching are fictional creations who only exist within the world of the play. What the playwrights are able to offer is an illusion of depth of character.

Even the language of a play offers an illusion of reality. When watching the characters speak in a naturalistic play, what they say strikes the audience as perfectly normal everyday speech. However, dramatic characters generally speak in turns, articulating what they want to say with very little effort. What they say is meaningful, logical and usually well-structured. There are very few of the stutters or false starts we would expect in a normal conversation; there are rarely periods of long silence; after all, five minutes of 'er', 'um' or 'No, after you!' would not make riveting viewing!

ACTIVITY 26

Key skills: communication: discussion

In groups of three:

1 One member of the group must act as note-taker, while the other two spend about two minutes describing to each other what they did last weekend. There should be some questioning from the listener (for example, 'What did you do then?' or 'Did you enjoy it?').

2 The note-taker must make a record of all the pauses, hesitations, repetitions and stutters featured in the conversation, as well as jotting down ideas as to how much sense the story is making! (If possible, you could also use a tape-recorder to play back the conversations to the whole group).

3 Rotate roles so you all spend some time as note-taker, then feed back to each other on how 'dramatically successful' the conversations were. How coherent were they? Were they easy to follow?

This should have given you a clear demonstration of the fact that we are very rarely able to produce a flawless dialogue in conversation. At any one time, you were having to think about three things at once – what you were saying, what you were going to say, and what your partner was saying, or how they were responding. This generally doesn't make for eloquent speaking! Clearly the language of naturalistic drama has to be more coherent and logically structured to make sense to an audience without them having to work too hard. Even when playwrights suggest pauses, repetitions and interruptions, their characters speak more fluently and are able to express more thoroughly what it is they want to say. How many times have you walked away from a conversation or disagreement, thinking 'If only I had said that …!'?

That said, the naturalistic dramatist must also provide an illusion of the thought-processes and aspects of real speech, otherwise it would be very difficult for the audience to believe that the characters were really responding spontaneously to each other. It is a good example of the way, as literature students, we must look 'behind the scenes' to the techniques which should, in performance, be almost unnoticeable. You will be looking behind the scenes in Activity 28.

People Talking To Themselves

Another good example of the way a dramatist creates an illusion through language is in the use of the *soliloquy*, a form of the *monologue*. We saw in the last chapter that, unlike a novel, unless naturalistic conventions are broken, there is no real way in which characters can reveal their thoughts and feelings on stage. However, the audience often needs such motives/feelings revealed, both to understand the plot and appreciate why the characters behave the way they do – a luxury we are definitely not given in everyday life.

Drama's answer to this is to bend the rules by allowing characters to talk to themselves at various points in the play; either when other people are present, in short asides to themselves and the audience (usually to reveal a brief opinion), or at length when they are on their own, as if they are thinking out loud. Often the characters the playwright gives such lines to are those we feel sympathy for. When we are given such an insight into their thoughts and feelings we feel an affinity for, and understanding of, the character. This can also allow for unusual twists; the villain of *Othello* (see the next chapter) is given more lines and soliloquys than Othello himself. This is perhaps one of the reasons why he is such an enthralling villain.

ACTIVITY 27

Key skills: communication – reading

1 Take any dramatic text you have studied so far and count:
   a) the number of words spoken by the each main character in one Act.
   b) the number of words the main characters speak to themselves.
This would probably work better with older

texts, which tend to use the aside/soliloquy more frequently than modern texts.

2 Discuss the results with a neighbour. Do the results back up the theory that it is the sympathetic characters who are given the most asides/soliloquys? If not, why not?

The aside and soliloquy are clearly *non*-naturalistic – you only have to watch its effect in certain modern American soap operas to realise this! However, even in such an obvious theatrical convention, the playwrights do their best to make the audience feel they are witnessing real thought-processes and emotions.

ACTIVITY 28

Key skills: communication – reading/discussion/ presentation

Individually, read the following examples of characters talking to themselves, making sure you fully understand them. Then:

1 Prepare a dramatic reading of one of the speeches, trying to make it sound as natural and realistic as possible. Concentrate on where you are going to pause; how you are going to portray any emotions expressed; and

how you are going to indicate changes of direction in the thought-process.

2 Once you have done this, underline all those aspects of the speech that seem to you to attempt to suggest a natural thought-process and everyday language. Indicate where you paused and try to work out why you paused at that specific point.

3 Perform your dramatic reading to the class, and then discuss aspects of the language which you feel allowed you to make it sound naturalistic.

Example A

(Juliet is about to take the potion given to her by Friar Lawrence, which will make her appear dead for forty-eight hours.)

JULIET: Farewell. God knows when we shall meet again.
I have a faint cold fear thrills through my veins
That almost freezes up the heat of life.
I'll call them back again to comfort me.
– Nurse! – What would she do here?
My dismal scene I needs must act alone.
Come, vial.
What if this mixture do not work at all?
Shall I be married then tomorrow morning?
No! No! This shall forbid it. Lie thou there.
(She lays down a knife)
What if it be a poison which the Friar
Subtly hath minister'd to have me dead,
Lest in this marriage he should be dishonoured,
Because he married me before to Romeo?
I fear it is. And yet methinks it should not,
For he hath still been tried a holy man.
How if, when I am laid into the tomb,
I wake before the time that Romeo
Come to redeem me? There's a fearful point!

Example B

(Doris has fallen off a chair while attempting to dust the top of a cabinet, injuring her leg. She is waiting for help to arrive.)

Pause.
Ought to have had a dog. Then it could have been barking for someone. Wilfred was always hankering after a dog. I wasn't keen. Hairs all up and down, then having to take it outside every five minutes. Wilfred said he would be prepared to undertake that responsibility. The dog would be his province. I said, 'Yes, and whose province would all the little hairs be?' I gave in in the finish, only I said it had to be on the small side. I didn't want one of them great lolloping, lamppost-smelling articles. And we never got one either. It was the growing mushrooms in the cellar saga all over again. He never got round to it. A kiddy'd've solved all that. Getting mad ideas. Like the fretwork, making toys and forts and whatnot. No end of money he was going to make. Then there was his phantom allotment. Oh, he was going to be coming home with leeks and spring cabbage and I don't know what. 'We can be self-sufficient in the vegetable department, Doris.' Never materialised. I was glad. It'd've meant muck somehow.
    Hello. Somebody coming. Salvation.

Example C

(On the instructions of her husband, Mrs Pinchwife is writing a letter to Mr Horner, in which she must inform him he is no longer to be her lover.)

'For Mr Horner.' – So, I am glad he has told me his name. Dear Mr Horner! But why should I send thee such a letter that will vex thee, and make thee angry with me? – Well, I will not send it. – Ay, but then my husband will kill me – for I see plainly he will not let me love Mr Horner – but what care I for my husband? – I won't, so I won't, send poor Mr Horner such a letter – But then my husband – but oh, what if I writ at bottom my husband made me write it? – Ay, but then my husband would see't – Can one have no shift? Ah, a London woman would have had a hundred presently. Stay – what if I should write a letter, and wrap it up like this, and write upon't too? Ay, but then my husband would see't – I don't know what to do. – But yet evads I'll try, so I will – for I will not send this letter to poor Mr Horner, come what will on't.

COMMENTARY

These three examples are clearly from very different periods of time: Example A is an extract from *Romeo and Juliet* by Shakespeare (1594), Example B from *A Cream Cracker Under the Settee* by Alan Bennett (1988), and Example C from *The Country Wife*, a Restoration Comedy by William Wycherley (1675). You no doubt immediately picked up on the fact that Shakespeare's extract is poetry, whereas the other two are prose – an important consideration, as we clearly don't all talk in iambic pentameter! Even so, you will perhaps have noticed how Shakespeare manages to make the rhythm very unobtrusive and close to the rhythms of real speech, so that Juliet's soliloquy still has an air of spontaneity about it. Of the three, you will no doubt have recognised that Bennett's extract imitates natural speech the most closely – no surprise, considering the relative dates of the three pieces. However, all three have aspects which are suggestive of immediate thought and everyday speech.

Example A

- A mixture of long and short sentences suggest different types of emotion and they follow the rhythms of natural speech rather than the line of poetry: 'No! No! This shall forbid it. Lie thou there.'
- Repeated questions suggest uncertainty and self-doubt.
- Exclamations of emotion – 'Nurse!' and 'There's a fearful point!'
- Repetition: 'No! No!'
- Juliet changes her mind, suggesting spontaneity: '– Nurse! – what would she do here?'

Example B

- Short sentences and sudden changes of direction suggest pauses for thought.
- There are a large number of minor sentences (sentences without a main verb); speech and writing follow different rules of grammar; and the extract contains a number of features of spoken language: 'Hairs all up and down, then having to take it outside every five minutes.'
- Elisions used are suggestive of speech: 'A kiddy'd've solved that'. Non-standard/informal language also suggests that the speech is immediate and spoken: 'I didn't want one of them great, lolloping, lamppost-smelling articles.'

Example C

■ A number of dashes suggest pauses and sudden ideas occurring to her.
■ There are a number of words suggestive of a provincial dialect: 'But yet evads I'll try, so I will ...'
■ Repetition of 'but then my husband ...' as each new idea is rejected suggests a spontaneity of ideas.
■ Mrs Pinchwife's final exclamation 'I don't know what to do' demonstrates the dilemma she is in.

Even though dramatic language, then, is a specific kind of language – structured, clear and generally logical – it nevertheless works hard to approximate to, and produce a version of, the language we use in everyday situations. Of course, this is as true when characters are talking to each other as it is when they are talking to themselves.

Dialogue: *The Crucible, Macbeth* and *The Birthday Party*

As we know, the 'Thespian' art is so-called because the Ancient Greek Thespis is reputed to have been the first to step away from the Chorus and interact with it, creating *dialogue* – and of course, although there is a place for the monologue (as Alan Bennett has shown), dialogue and interaction between characters could be said to be the 'bread and butter' of the theatre.

Emotion on stage does not simply occur naturally; it is created through an intricate interaction between pauses and language, action and speech, and silence and noise, to name a few. The actor then has an even wider repertoire of techniques to convey the emotion – what are known in language study as *paralinguistic* features: that is, aspects of the dialogue that are not linguistic, but act as an accompaniment to the words: facial expression, body language and movement around the stage. But the initial emotion is created by the language and often the dramatist's stage directions are very specific about what the actors should do and when. What characters say to each other is a matter of plot and character; but the way in which they say it; the speed at which they say things; and what they do in between saying them, all of these aspects need to be considered by the playwright, as they are the major aspect of the drama that takes place and the effect it has on the audience.

Tempo

Many of these aspects of the dialogue affect the tempo, or pace, of the piece of drama. This is something more obvious in performance than reading, perhaps, but something you need to be aware of, as it is an important aspect of it. Individual scenes will need a certain tempo suited to their content; and if the tempo of the whole play is too fast or too slow for too long, the audience will soon be either exhausted, or bored, and switch off!

ACTIVITY 29

Key skills: communication – writing/discussion/presentation

1 In pairs, create a list of the aspects of a dialogue that could either create a fast or slow tempo. Think about such things as sentence lengths and types of sentence, and also whether any paralinguistic features will influence the speed of the scene.

2 Now write two short drama scripts based around the well-known scenario of the bank robbery. In the first one, use the techniques you have identified to make the tempo fast and exciting; in the second, make the tempo slow and leisurely. The characters you create in each may affect the pace, but also focus on aspects of dialogue in creating its tempo.

3 Perform your scripts!

ACTIVITY 30

Key skills: communication – reading/discussion

With a different partner, read the following extract from Arthur Miller's *The Crucible* (1953), a conversation between John Proctor and his wife Elizabeth, and then discuss:

1 How fast did you find yourself reading the scene? Would the scene have been faster, or slower, if you had acted it out with props?

2 How would you describe the atmosphere in this scene? Calm? Relaxed? Tense?

3 What is the importance of Miller's detailed stage directions concerning the serving and eating of the food? How do they add to the atmosphere of the scene?

4 Look at the length of the lines each character says. What does this suggest about their relationship?

ELIZABETH: What keeps you so late? It's almost dark.
PROCTOR: I were planting far out to the forest edge.
ELIZABETH: Oh, you're done, then.
PROCTOR: Ay, the farm is seeded. The boys asleep?
ELIZABETH: They will be soon. *(And she goes to the fireplace, proceeds to ladle up stew in a dish.)*
PROCTOR: Pray now for a fair summer.
ELIZABETH: Aye.
PROCTOR: Are you well today?
ELIZABETH: I am. *(She brings the plate to the table, and, indicating the food)* It is a rabbit.
PROCTOR: *(going to the table)* Oh, is it! In Jonathan's trap?
ELIZABETH: No, she walked into the house this afternoon; I found her sittin' in the corner like she come to visit.
PROCTOR: Oh, that's a good sign walkin' in.
ELIZABETH: Pray God. It hurt my heart to strip her, poor rabbit. *(She sits and watches him taste it.)*
PROCTOR: It's well seasoned.
ELIZABETH: *(blushing with pleasure)* I took great care. She's tender?
PROCTOR: Aye. *(He eats. She watches him.)* I think we'll see green fields soon. It's warm as blood beneath the clods.
ELIZABETH: That's well.
(Proctor eats, then looks up.)

PROCTOR: If the crop is good I'll buy George Jacob's heifer. How would that please you?
ELIZABETH: Aye, it would.
PROCTOR: *(with a grin)* I mean to please you, Elizabeth.
ELIZABETH: *(it is hard to say)* I know it, John.
(He gets up, goes to her, kisses her. She receives it. With a certain disappointment, he returns to the table.)

The Crucible, Arthur Miller, (1953)

COMMENTARY

What should have struck you immediately about this scene is that the tempo is very slow. The short, often abrupt sentences, and the pauses during which the meal is served and eaten, with the silences they create, all suggest an atmosphere of tension, with the conversation seeming stilted and awkward. Notice that it is Proctor who tries to create a conversation, asking numerous questions and raising the weather, the farm and the fact that he is looking to buy a heifer. Elizabeth answers him abruptly, sometimes monosyllabically, not taking the bait and instead making Proctor work in the dialogue. Proctor is clearly trying to make up for something – the ending of the extract gives this away, with John saying 'I mean to please you' – and then particularly in the very deliberate movement in which Elizabeth 'receives' (but does not respond to) his kiss, and he turns away in disappointment. However, this only confirms the atmosphere of recrimination and awkwardness which the dialogue has created from the opening of the scene. In fact, the audience already know that John has had an affair, as the information has been revealed in the previous Act.

ACTIVITY 31

Key skills: communication – reading

The following extract is tense for very different reasons. It is night-time and Macbeth has just gone to murder his sleeping King. His wife, Lady Macbeth, waits for him in the courtyard of their castle.

1 Identify the tempo of this scene. Should it be fast or slow? Are there points at which the tempo changes? Why?
2 Look at Lady Macbeth's opening speech and Macbeth's speech nearer the end of the extract. Jot down notes about how you would deliver this in performance. Think about pace, pauses and any paralinguistic features which could go with the words.
3 Look at the lengths of the sentences from line 20 onwards. What do they suggest about the way each character is dealing with the situation?

Enter LADY MACBETH

LADY M: That which hath made them drunk hath made me bold:	1
What hath quenched them hath given me fire – Hark! – Peace!	
It was the owl that shriek'd, the fatal bellman,	
Which gives the stern'st good-night. He is about it.	
The doors are open, and the surfeited grooms	5
Do mock their charge with snores: I have drugged their possets,	possets: drinks
That Death and Nature do contend about them,	
Whether they live, or die.	

MACB: (within) Who's there? – what, ho!
LADY M: Alack! I am afraid they have awak'd,   10
And 'tis not done: – th'attempt and not the deed
Confounds us. –Hark! – I laid their daggers ready;
He could not miss 'em. – Had he not resembled
My father as he slept, I had done't. My husband!
Enter MACBETH
MACB: I have done the deed. – Didst thou not hear a noise?   15
LADY M: I heard the owl scream, and the crickets cry.
Did not you speak?
MACB: When?
LADY M: Now.
MACB: As I descended?
LADY M: Ay.
MACB: Hark!
Who lies i'th'second chamber?
LADY M: Donalbain.
MACB: This is a sorry sight.   20
LADY M: A foolish thought, to say a sorry sight.
MACB: There's one did cry in's sleep, and one cried, 'Murther!'
That they did wake each other: I stood and heard them;
But they did say their prayers, and addressed them
Again to sleep.
LADY M: There are two lodg'd together.
MACB: One cried 'God bless us!' and, 'Amen,' the other,   25
As they had seen me with these hangman's hands.
List'ning their fear, I could not say, 'Amen',
When they did say, 'God bless us.'
LADY M: Consider it not so deeply.
MACB: But wherefore could I not pronounce 'Amen'?
I had most need of blessing, and 'Amen'
Stuck in my throat.   30
LADY M: These deeds must not be thought
After these ways: so, it will make us mad.

Macbeth, Act II, sc. ii, ll. 1–31

COMMENTARY Your notes on Lady Macbeth's opening soliloquy may well have looked
something like this:

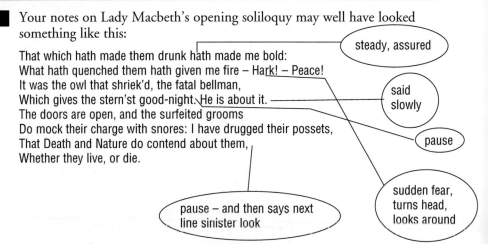

That which hath made them drunk hath made me bold:
What hath quenched them hath given me fire – Hark! – Peace!
It was the owl that shriek'd, the fatal bellman,
Which gives the stern'st good-night. He is about it.
The doors are open, and the surfeited grooms
Do mock their charge with snores: I have drugged their possets,
That Death and Nature do contend about them,
Whether they live, or die.

steady, assured

said slowly

pause

sudden fear, turns head, looks around

pause – and then says next line sinister look

Even if you had read these lines differently, it is clear that within this short
number of lines, there are a number of changes of tempo as Lady

Macbeth's thoughts change. You may have based some of your interpretation on the punctuation of the speech. It is worth knowing that most aspects of punctuation are the work of modern editors: as there were no hard and fast rules governing the presentation of English in Shakespeare's time, there were very few punctuation marks in the original text.

Nevertheless, the editors base their punctuation on the meaning of the lines, and the sense demands a pause of some sort before Lady Macbeth says 'He is about it' (perhaps as she looks fearfully around the courtyard), whereas the exclamations '– Hark! – Peace!' suggest speed as she reacts to the hooting of an owl. Similarly, the flurry of exchanges between Macbeth and Lady Macbeth on lines 16–20 suggest speed, and there is a clear contrast between Macbeth's longer, dreamy lines and Lady Macbeth's terse replies on lines 20–31.

The last extract you are going to look at in this section is from one of the more recent masters of dialogue, Harold Pinter. It has been said that 'the new patterns of dialogue can be regarded as the principal interest of each [Pinter] play'; and Pinter's style is so distinctive that the adjective 'Pinteresque' has been created to refer to the kind of dialogue he creates. The following exchange is relatively typical of Pinter's uniquely individual form of dialogue. It is also very different from any of the extracts you have looked at so far.

ACTIVITY 32

Key skills: communication – reading/discussion

Read, and then discuss, the following extract from *The Birthday Party* by Harold Pinter (1958). Consider:

a the tempo of the piece, and the way this tempo is created

b how naturalistic you consider the piece to be – in other words, how close it is to an everyday conversation

c whether there is a rhythm or pattern to the dialogue in the extract. If so, how does it add to the meaning of the scene?

d what the tone of the extract is – serious, comic, frightening? How does the language create this tone?

e how the stage directions concerning movement add to the effect of the scene.

Two men, Goldberg and McCann, have arrived mysteriously and unannounced at the boarding house where Stanley Webber lives. Now he is on his own, they begin to question him.

GOLDBERG: Take off his glasses.
(McCANN snatches his glasses and as STANLEY rises, reaching for them, takes his chair downstage centre, below the table, STANLEY fumbling as he follows. STANLEY clutches the chair and stays bent over it.)
Webber, you're a fake. *(They stand on each side of the chair.)*
When did you last wash up a cup?
STANLEY: The Christmas before last.
GOLDBERG: Where?
STANLEY: Lyons Corner House.
GOLDBERG: Which one?

STANLEY: Marble Arch.
GOLDBERG: Where was your wife?
STANLEY: In –
GOLDBERG: Answer.
STANLEY *(turning, crouched)*: What wife?
GOLDBERG: What have you done with your wife?
McCANN: He's killed his wife!
GOLDBERG: Why did you kill your wife?
STANLEY *(sitting, his back to the audience)*: What wife?
McCANN: How did he kill her?
GOLDBERG: How did you kill her?
McCANN: You throttled her.
GOLDBERG: With arsenic.
McCANN: There's your man!
GOLDBERG: Where's your old mum?
STANLEY: In the sanatorium.
McCANN: Yes!
GOLDBERG: Why did you never get married?
McCANN: She was waiting at the porch.
GOLDBERG: You skedaddled from the wedding.
McCANN: He left her in the lurch.
GOLDBERG: You left her in the pudding club.
McCANN: She was waiting at the church.
GOLDBERG: Webber! Why did you change your name?
STANLEY: I forgot the other one.
GOLDBERG: What's your name now?
STANLEY: Joe Soap.
GOLDBERG: You stink of sin.
McCANN: I can smell it.
GOLDBERG: Do you recognise an external force?
STANLEY: What?
GOLDBERG: Do you recognise an external force?
McCANN: That's the question!
GOLDBERG: Do you recognise an external force, responsible for you, suffering for you?
STANLEY: It's late!
GOLDBERG: Late! Late enough! When did you last pray?
McCANN: He's sweating!
GOLDBERG: When did you last pray?
McCANN: He's sweating!

The Birthday Party, Harold Pinter (1958)

COMMENTARY　The immediately striking aspect of this dialogue is how nonsensical much of it is. Goldberg and McCann take the role of interrogators (helped visually by the fact they stand over Stanley, who is 'bent' in the chair), but their questions are bizarre, contradictory and illogical. Goldberg asks 'What have you done with your wife?', a bemused Stanley asks 'What wife?', and only a few lines later Goldberg again asks 'Why did you never get married?' The confusion is increased by the repetition of questions in the second (you) and third (he) person, and the *juxtaposition* (placing together for contrast) of seemingly contradictory statements:

McCANN: How did he kill her?

GOLDBERG: How did you kill her?
McCANN: You throttled her.
GOLDBERG: With arsenic.

The short, quickfire questions and statements (a *stichomythic* style, the term meaning a quick flurry of exchanges – see Chapter 2, page 25) of the interrogation also create a very fast tempo which would further disorientate an audience (as it does Stanley), and a pattern of rhymes and a childish rhythm almost give the extract a riddle-like quality:

McCANN: She was waiting at the *porch*.
GOLDBERG: You ske*daddl*ed from the we*dd*ing.
McCANN: He left her in the *lurch*.
GOLDBERG: You left her in the p*u*dding cl*u*b.
McCANN: She was waiting at the *church*.

Ronald Hayman has said that Harold Pinter 'has capitalised in a way … on the fact that real-life conversations don't proceed smoothly and logically from point to point'. However, the effect in this extract is so confusing as to be entirely non-naturalistic, as the questions themselves are meaningless and seem to rely as much on sound as sense. Goldberg and McCann are asking questions simply because they can ask questions, something that becomes even more apparent later in the interrogation:

GOLDBERG: Speak up, Webber. Why did the chicken cross the road?
STANLEY: He wanted to – he wanted to – he wanted to …
McCANN: He doesn't know!
GOLDBERG: Why did the chicken cross the road?
STANLEY: He wanted to – he wanted to …
GOLDBERG: Why did the chicken cross the road?
STANLEY: He wanted …
McCANN: He doesn't know. He doesn't know which came first!
GOLDBERG: Which came first?
McCANN: Chicken? Egg? Which came first?

The questions asked are clearly absurd but also somehow terrifying (in response to these questions, '(*STANLEY screams*)'). Their pace and inevitability demand answers so perhaps the scene is saying something about the nature of language and authority (although Pinter is quick to dissociate himself from intending any one 'meaning': he wrote of the play, 'The thing germinated and bred itself'). The bizarre nature of the extract is very similar to the *absurdist* drama of writers such as Beckett and Ionesco, which lends itself well to a post-structuralist analysis – an example is given of an extract from Beckett in Chapter 5.

Plot structure

From the early days of theatre, attempts have been made to set rules as to the structure of drama and equal numbers of dramatists have flagrantly flouted them. Following Aristotle's descriptions of Greek Tragedy in the fourth century BC, critics and dramatists of the sixteenth and seventeenth centuries identified three unifying principles in 'good' drama, the *dramatic unities*:

- A drama should concern one story only, with no distracting subplots (unity of *action*)
- The action should take place in one setting only (*unity of place*)
- The action should be continuous and take place in the space of a day (*unity of time*).

However, more plays are conspicuous for not following these unities than for following them and, typically, the (mainly French) writers who insisted on the superiority of the unities were the ones who used them in their plays – for example, Jean Racine. (A good recent example of an English play that does follow the unities is *An Inspector Calls,* by J. B. Priestley.)

In the nineteenth century, a type of play emerged in France called *pièce bien faite* – known as the 'well-made play' – so called because of the neatly constructed plots which built efficiently towards dramatic *dénouements* (or climaxes) in which all loose ends were tied up. Such a tradition continued in England into the twentieth century with writers like Terence Rattigan, but the polished plot development soon became associated with superficial sheen; and after watching the first performance of the loosely structured (and revolutionary) *Look Back in Anger* by John Osborne, Rattigan suggested the play should have been retitled 'Look how unlike Terence Rattigan I am being.'

The fact that so many dramatists (including Shakespeare) have paid little attention to imposed notions of 'good structure' demonstrates that there is no one 'correct' structure for a play to have. That said, clearly the way a playwright organises and structures a plot can have a dramatic effect on the audience. Flashbacks, soliloquys, and pieces of information revealed at specific moments can all affect an audience's perceptions of a play and, as we have already seen, the playwright can skilfully manipulate the audience's emotions through such things as tempo and tension. However, tempo and tension are not just important to individual scenes; the pattern of tense and relaxed moments and fast and slow scenes can influence an audience's overall response to a play.

As an example, the extracts you have read from *The Crucible* and *Macbeth* represent two highly tense scenes. However, each extract is different: *The Crucible*'s tension arises from the awkwardness of John and Elizabeth's relations, has a slow tempo and is very quiet, with a number of pauses; whereas the extract from *Macbeth* is highly dramatic and generally faster, as Lady Macbeth and Macbeth meet after Duncan's murder. It is worth considering these extracts in their contexts within the play. The extract from *The Crucible* follows on from a highly dramatic, up-tempo, loud scene in which the girls name the Salem 'witches'; and the scene from *Macbeth* is followed by a long, slow, rambling and comic speech from a porter as he goes to open the castle gates.

ACTIVITY 33

Key skills: communication – discussion

Why might Shakespeare and Arthur Miller have *juxtaposed* (placed next to each other for contrast) such different scenes in this way? What effect would this have on the audience?

COMMENTARY The juxtaposition of such scenes modulates the audience's emotions and gives them chance to 'take a breath' after a highly tense or emotional section. We have all seen the kind of horror film in which the typically foolish hero or heroine approaches a haunted house at night and all the usual 'suspense' elements are employed: creaking floorboards, bats, rats and the like. However, now imagine that the level of suspense were kept up for the full length of the film, and then the credits rolled. You would probably respond in two ways:

i You would feel cheated that the tension and suspense created did not lead to anything, so the emotions that had developed were not released;

ii You may well 'switch off' after a fairly short amount of time – there is only so much suspense and tension we can take before becoming 'desensitised' because of overload.

This demonstrates the importance of the dramatist carefully structuring the action of the play so that the audience's emotions are heightened, but never over-wrought. This has been one of the explanations for comic scenes in otherwise highly tense tragedies; they provide *comic relief* and give the audience time to recover, ready for the next 'assault' on their senses. As Macbeth says, 'I have supped full with horrors:/Direness, familiar to my slaughterous thoughts,/Cannot once start me.' Through patterning the scenes to create a mixture of emotions, the playwright can make sure this doesn't happen to the audience.

If we were to take the structure of *The Crucible* in its entirety, we would see the way the plot is carefully constructed to create contrasting tension and relaxation for the audience through juxtaposing scenes:

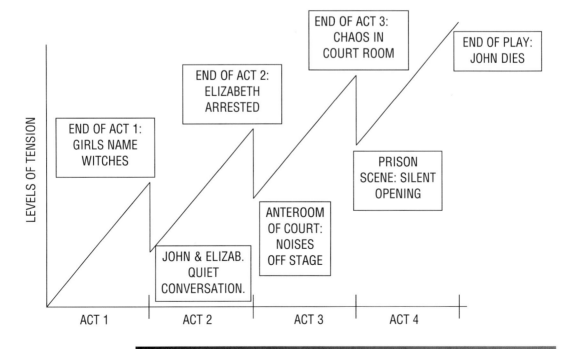

ACTIVITY 34

Key skills: communication – reading

Working on your own, take a dramatic text you know well and attempt to plot a chart similar to that done above for *The Crucible*. Identify fast and slow scenes and then decide which may be more emotionally demanding for the audience. Is there a pattern to the way the playwright has structured the scenes to elicit a response from the audience?

Comedy: *The Rivals* and *Absurd Person Singular*

So far we have focused on 'serious' drama and the effect it has on an audience. However, as Alan Ayckbourn has written, 'As a nation, we show a marked preference for comedy when it comes to playgoing, as any theatre manager will tell you'; and we are going to spend some time now considering not what creates tension and stress in an audience, but what makes them laugh.

ACTIVITY 35

Key skills: communication – research/discussion/documents

1 Over the following week, keep a 'comedy diary' of all the things that make you laugh, whether it is read in a book or magazine, heard in a conversation or watched on television. If possible, note down or cut out the actual item.
2 Get together in groups and compare your results. Did you all find the same things amusing? Did the items you had found represent different types of comedy? How many would work in the theatre?
3 Produce a wall-chart to demonstrate the different types of things that can make people laugh, using examples from the items you have kept or recorded.

COMMENTARY   Comedy can come from a variety of different sources and what one person finds hysterical may leave another person cold. However, the four most common sources of humour are probably:

- characters (for example, Victor Meldrew)
- language (wordplay)
- situations (which often provoke amusing character responses – the modern TV 'sitcom', or situation comedy, is based on amusing situations which people find themselves in)
- visual humour (somebody pulling a funny face, or slipping on a banana skin – known as 'slapstick').

ACTIVITY 36

**Key skills: communication –
reading/discussion**

The following extract is from Richard
Sheridan's *The Rivals* (1775). In pairs, read the extract and then decide where its humour lies. Does the dialogue offer any opportunities for actors to create humour through gestures or other paralinguistic features?

(Acres has issued the challenge of a duel to Beverley, his rival for the hand of Lydia Languish. He has sent for his friend, Captain Jack Absolute, to deliver the challenge, not realising Captain Absolute is secretly Beverley – something we the audience already know.)

Enter SERVANT

SERVANT: Captain Absolute, sir. *(Exit servant)*
ACRES: Oh, show him up.
DAVID: Well, heaven send we may all be alive this time tomorrow!
ACRES: What's that? Don't provoke me, David!
DAVID: *(whimpering)* Goodbye, master.
ACRES: Get along, you cowardly, dastardly, croaking raven.
(Exit David)
Enter CAPTAIN ABSOLUTE
ABSOLUTE: What's the matter, Bob?
ACRES: A vile, sheep-hearted blockhead! If I hadn't the valour of St George and the Dragon to boot –
ABSOLUTE: But what did you want with me, Bob?
ACRES: *(Producing letter)* Oh! There –
ABSOLUTE: *(Reading)* 'To Ensign Beverley.' So. *(Aside)* What's going on now! Well, what's this?
ACRES: A challenge!
ABSOLUTE: But what have I to do with this?
ACRES: Why, as you know something of this fellow, I want you to find him out for me and give him this mortal defiance.
ABSOLUTE: Well, give it to me, and trust me he gets it.
ACRES: You are very kind. What it is to have a friend! You couldn't be my second, could you, Jack?
ABSOLUTE: Why, no, Bob – not in this affair. – It would not be quite so proper.
ACRES: Well, then, I must get my friend Sir Lucius. I shall have your good wishes, however, Jack?
ABSOLUTE: Whenever he meets you, believe me.
Enter SERVANT
SERVANT: Sir Anthony Absolute is below, inquiring for the Captain.
ABSOLUTE: *(Rising)* I'll come instantly. Well, my little hero, success attend you.
ACRES: Stay – stay, Jack. If Beverley should ask you what kind of a man your friend Acres is, tell him I am a devil of a fellow – will you, Jack?
ABSOLUTE: To be sure, I shall. I'll say you are a determined dog, hey, Bob?
ACRES: Aye, do, do – and if that frightens him, perhaps he mayn't come. So tell him I generally kill a man a week: will you, Jack?
ABSOLUTE: *(Going)* I will, I will.
ACRES: Remember, Jack, a determined dog!
ABSOLUTE: Aye, aye, 'Fighting Bob!'

The Rivals, Sheridan (1775)

COMMENTARY Clearly much of the humour of this extract comes from the *dramatic irony* of the fact that the audience is aware of Absolute's double identity, whereas Acres isn't. Acres is clearly terrified at the prospect of the duel, not helped by David's comically pessimistic comments and this is something which an actor could make much of on the stage, particularly when Acres pretends to have 'the valour of St George and the Dragon' and his asking Absolute to pretend 'I generally kill a man a week' when in fact Absolute is his rival. This is clearly rich in comedy. Absolute himself realises this and makes a number of ironic comments – 'Well, give it to me, and trust me he gets it'. His parting reference to 'Fighting Bob' leaves the audience in no doubt as to where the humour lies. Of course, an actor could well use facial expressions to indicate his amusement to an audience. In many ways, this is an early example of situation comedy – Absolute's double identity creates the humorous situation. However, character is also a rich source of humour here, with Acres and David both terrified yet attempting to bluff bravery!

ACTIVITY 37

Key skills: communication – reading/discussion

In the following extract from Alan Ayckbourn's *Absurd Person Singular*, Sidney and Jane Hopcroft and Ronald and Marion Brewster-Wright have visited Geoffrey and Eva Jackson at their flat. The action takes place in the kitchen, where a light fitting has been broken and is being fixed by Ronald.

1 In groups, prepare a performance of the scene. It doesn't have to be polished; just work out where the characters would stand and move at various points in the extract.
2 Watch the performances, and then as a class discuss the humour of the scene. Compare its humour to that found in *The Rivals*. How similar is it?

RONALD: Blast.
SIDNEY: What's the matter?
RONALD: Dropped the little thing. Could you see if you can see it? I've got to keep holding onto this or it'll drop off. Little thing about so big.
MARION: What little thing?
RONALD: A whajamacallit.
JANE: Small, was it?
RONALD: Lord, yes. Tiny little thing.
SIDNEY: Oh dear oh dear.
(They hunt. Sidney crawls on his hands and knees)
JANE: Might have rolled anywhere.
MARION: What are we looking for?
RONALD: Little whosit. Goes in here.
MARION: Darling, do be more precise. What's a whosit?
JANE: You know, one of those – one of those – isn't that silly, I can't think of the word.
MARION: Well, I refuse to look till I know what we're looking for. I mean, from the look of this floor it's simply littered with little whosits.
SIDNEY: *(under the table)* Can't see it.
JANE: It's on the lip of my tongue … that's it, a nut. Little nut.
MARION: *(searching by the sink)* Oh, well, then, a nut. Now we know. Everyone hunt for a little nut.
(Eva goes and sits at the table)

SIDNEY: I didn't know we were looking for a nut.
JANE: Aren't we?
RONALD: No. A screw. That's what I'm after. A screw.
SIDNEY: A screw, yes.
JANE: Oh, a screw.
MARION: All right, everybody, stop looking for nuts. Ronnie's now decided he wants a screw. I can't see a thing. And I think it would be terribly sensible if we put the light on, wouldn't it?
RONALD: Good idea.
(Marion goes to the light switch)
SIDNEY: *(realising far too late)* No, I wouldn't turn that on ...
(Marion presses the switch)
MARION: There.
(Ronald, on the table, starts vibrating, emitting a low moan)
SIDNEY: *(rising)* Turn it off.
JANE: Get him away.
MARION: Darling, what on earth are you doing?
JANE: *(reaching out to pull Ronald away)* Get him away.
SIDNEY: No, don't touch him, he's live. *(He goes to the switch)*
(Jane touches him and recoils, with a squeak)
RONALD: *(through gritted teeth)* Somebody turn it off.
(Sidney turns it off)
SIDNEY: All right. Panic over.
(Ronald continues to vibrate)

Absurd Person Singular, Ayckbourn (1972)

COMMENTARY   There is comedy of character, with Ronald attempting to bluff his knowledge of DIY with terms like 'whajamacallit', clearly demonstrating the fact that he has no real idea. Just as Acres attempted to bluff his bravery, Ronald clearly wants to appear the 'man in control', something undermined by the fact that his wife seems to have far more practical sense! The situation also is a comic one, with the misunderstanding leading to Ronald becoming 'live', something which has vast visual potential, as he 'continues to vibrate' after Sidney has announced 'Panic over'. Notice how the short sentence lengths add to the humour, particularly in the way they portray Ronald's incompetence: 'Little whosit. Goes in here.'

There are also verbal jokes in the extract – 'Ronnie's now decided he wants a screw' may seem like an obvious *double entendre*, but has a more subtle irony when we remember he has just revealed he is leaving his wife for another woman – and the play as a whole is a satire on sexual infidelity within marriage. In many ways, the humour is very similar to that of *The Rivals* – we enjoy watching people make fools of themselves in ludicrous situations. Although fashions have changed and there have been superficial differences in taste, it is safe to say we have been finding the same things funny since the time of Aristophanes in Ancient Greece!

Characterisation: Who's Afraid of Virginia Woolf?

Earlier, we considered the fact that A. C. Bradley's famous mistake in responding to Shakespeare's plays was the way in which he described them as living, breathing people with a life and existence beyond that of the play, when in actual fact they were dramatic constructions.

That said, clearly Shakespeare had created the illusion of real life characters so well that Bradley felt he knew them as real people and, certainly in naturalistic drama, we are meant to respond to characters as real, living people. Imagine a piece of drama which is purely one of ideas – if it were possible for it to exist, it might be said it would not be particularly enthralling!

Often playwrights write plays to express specific ideas and themes, but there is a significance in that they chose to express their ideas through drama. It is not a political tract or piece of philosophy and the characters are the means by which those ideas begin to 'live'. Aristotle recognised their importance when he wrote 'Character is Destiny'.

We should certainly be aware of the craft by which a playwright creates character; but if a playwright has gone to so much trouble to create an illusion of people with real existences, then it seems rather mean-spirited for us to sit there and refuse to see them as anything other than 'dramatic constructions'. We need to perform a mental feat which, after George Orwell, we could call 'doublethink': responding strongly to the characters as individuals as an audience would, but also (and preferably, simultaneously) being able to see the way the dramatist has created the illusion of reality. When a character pauses for thought, we need to be able to imagine what they are thinking, while also realising the impossibility of them thinking anything!

Characterisation, past and present

The concept of responding to a character as an 'individual' is in fact a relatively new concept in English drama. In medieval drama (see page 27), 'characters' only existed as personifications of Biblical characters or abstract concepts (for example, the Seven Deadly Sins). They were what we could call types, with little to suggest they possessed individual traits or ideas. Christopher Marlowe was one of the first playwrights to give a greater sense of individuality to his characters, although even then they still held some symbolic value (Faustus representing the 'over-reacher' from the morality plays and Barrabas the *Machiavellian* villain). Similar types existed in Shakespeare's plays, although he took the characterisation one step further creating depths of motive and thought and often playing with the very types themselves – a comparison of Shakespeare's Shylock with Marlowe's Barrabas demonstrates as much.

Even during the Restoration period, characters were presented as types. Although given individual thoughts and ideas, the characters tended to fall into categories; the faithless young wife, the irresponsible elder son, the gold-digging young man and the old, lusty widow appear time and again in Restoration Comedies (for a further discussion of these, see pages 35). Often their very names indicate their type: for example, Colonel Bully and Lady Fanciful in John Vanbrugh's *The Provoked Wife*, or Thomas Aimwell and Lady Bountiful in George Farquhar's *The Beaux Stratagem*.

It was only with the advent of naturalism in the nineteenth century (see pages 37) that characters were finally portrayed as living, thinking people, something owing as much to language as anything else. No longer speaking in poetry, or in the mannered word-play of Restoration Comedy, characters could speak in a form that appeared to the audience as natural and spontaneous. This has now become the generally accepted form of theatre, something increased by the even greater naturalism we are offered in television drama.

ACTIVITY 38

Key skills: communication – reading/discussion

In groups of four, read the following extract from the modern play *Who's Afraid of Virginia Woolf?* by Edward Albee, and discuss how you think it should be performed. Then, consider the following:

1 How does Albee create a sense of these characters having a past?
2 How does Albee suggest the characters are thinking and speaking spontaneously?
3 Now each take the character you acted and

make notes on their character as they appear in this extract. Consider such things as:

a what they say (and what it suggests about them);
b the relationships they have with the others;
c how important Albee's acting instructions are in creating their character.
Find quotations to back up the points you make.

4 Feed back to the rest of your group on your character. Discuss whether other members of the group saw them in a different light.

(*A young couple, Nick and Honey, have returned to the house of Martha and George after meeting them at a campus party. Nick is a young lecturer; George a senior lecturer. Honey has just returned from being sick, rather the worse for wear with drink.*)

HONEY: *(grandly)* Thank you ... thank you.
MARTHA: Here we are, a little shaky, but on our feet.
GEORGE: Goodie.
NICK: What? Oh ... OH! Hi, Honey ... you better?
HONEY: A little bit, dear ... I'd better sit down, though.
NICK: Sure ... c'mon ... you sit by me.
HONEY: Thank you, dear.
GEORGE: *(beneath his breath)*: Touching ... touching.
MARTHA: *(to GEORGE)* Well? Aren't you going to apologise?
GEORGE: *(squinting)* For what, Martha?
MARTHA: For making the little lady throw up, what else?
GEORGE: I did not make her throw up.
MARTHA: You most certainly did.
GEORGE: I did not!

HONEY *(papal gesture)*: No, now ... no.
MARTHA: *(to George)* Well, who do you think did ... Sexy over there? You think he made his *own* little wife sick?
GEORGE: *(helpfully)* Well, you make *me* sick.
MARTHA: THAT'S DIFFERENT!
HONEY: No, now. I ... I throw up ... I mean, I get sick ... occasionally, all by myself ... without any reason.
GEORGE: Is that a fact?
NICK: You're ... you're delicate, Honey.
HONEY: *(proudly)* I've always done it.
GEORGE: Like Big Ben.
NICK: *(a warning)* Watch it!
HONEY: And the doctors say there's nothing wrong with me ... organically. You know?
NICK: Of course there isn't.
HONEY: Why, just before we got married, I developed ... appendicitis ... or everybody *thought* it was appendicitis ... but it turned out to be ... it was a ... *(Laughs briefly)* ... false alarm.
(George and Nick exchange glances)
MARTHA: *(to George)* Get me a drink.

Who's Afraid of Virginia Woolf?, Edward Albee (1962)

COMMENTARY

One of the inevitable problems in providing extracts in this way is what we can call the 'bleeding chunks' syndrome: there is a lot going on in this extract (for example, Nick and George's glance) that relates to other parts of the play, and to read only this one severed extract does not do it full justice. However, rather than reveal to you the way in which certain elements relate to the whole play, I can only suggest you discover it for yourself, either through reading, performance or watching the excellent film adaptation starring Richard Burton and Elizabeth Taylor.

That said, there is still a considerable amount we can draw from the extract in terms of character analysis. Albee is very generous with his directions, leaving us in no doubt as to the way in which the characters behave: 'HONEY: *(proudly)* I've always done it.' The characters are also very strong (and react violently to each other) and are presented very naturalistically, so we can almost believe that Honey did, at some point, have suspected appendicitis. War-weary Martha and George also give the impression of having been together for a very long time – too long, perhaps! Notice the way that Albee suggests the characters are talking and thinking spontaneously: the pauses in Honey's speech create the illusion of confused thought and there is her almost unconscious self-correction of 'throw up' to 'get sick' (perhaps because George is Nick's work superior and she wants to appear polite).

ACTIVITY 39

Key skills: communication – discussion

Watch this extract as performed in the film version of *Who's Afraid of Virginia Woolf?* starring Richard Burton and Elizabeth Taylor, then discuss whether you agreed with the way the scene was played. Were there any major differences with the way you had envisioned it being performed?

Stagecraft

So far we have been considering plays which have been naturalistic, at least in the sense that the world they create on stage follows the same physical rules as would happen in real life and the characters are unaware of the fact that they are dramatic constructions – they believe in their own existence and follow the physical rules of the world the playwright has created.

That being the case, so far we have taken the stage area itself for granted, focusing only on what the characters say (and, more peripherally, how they might move to suggest it). However, the way in which a playwright makes use of the staging and physical aspects of a performance – stagecraft – can often be equally important to its effect, something more obvious when the use of the stage is unusual or out of the ordinary. The following two extracts are from the openings of twentieth century plays. The first extract provides the opening stage directions and the second the opening monologue. Both demonstrate a strikingly unusual use of stagecraft.

ACTIVITY 40

Key skills: communication – reading

For the next two extracts, consider the unusual use the playwrights have made of different aspects of performance. To what extent can these aspects be said to have a symbolic meaning (do they represent something)? How do the openings differ from the conventions of naturalistic drama?

A melody is heard, played upon a flute. It is small and fine, telling of grass and trees and the horizon. The curtain rises.

Before us is the Salesman's house. We are aware of towering, angular shapes behind it, surrounding it on all sides. Only the blue light of the sky falls upon the house and forestage; the surrounding area shows an angry glow of orange. As more light appears we see a solid vault of apartment houses around the small, fragile seeming home. An air of the dream clings to the place, a dream rising out of reality. The kitchen at centre seems actual enough, for there is a kitchen table with three chairs, and a refrigerator. But no other fixtures are seen. At the back of the kitchen is a draped entrance, which leads to the living room. To the right of the kitchen, on a level raised two feet, is a bedroom furnished only with a brass bedstead and a straight chair. On a shelf over the bed a silver athletic trophy stands. A window opens onto the apartment house at the side.

Behind the kitchen, on a level raised six and a half feet, is the boys' bedroom, at present barely visible. Two beds are dimly seen, and at the back of the room a dormer window. (This bedroom is above the unseen living-room.) At the left a stairway curves up to it from the kitchen.

The entire setting is wholly or, in some places, partially transparent. The roof-line of the house is one-dimensional; under and over it we see the apartment buildings. Before the house lies an apron, curving beyond the forestage into the orchestra. This forward area serves as the back yard as well as the locale of all Willy's imaginings and of his city scenes. Whenever the action is in the present the actors observe the imaginary wall lines, entering the house only through its door at the left. But in the scenes of the past these boundaries are broken, and characters enter or leave a room by stepping 'through a wall' onto the forestage.

From the right, WILLY LOMAN, the salesman, enters, carrying two large sample cases. The flute plays on. He hears but is not aware of it. He is past sixty years of age, dressed quietly. Even as he crosses the stage to the doorway of the house, his exhaustion is apparent.

Death of a Salesman, Arthur Miller (1949)

TOM: Yes, I have tricks in my pocket, I have things up my sleeve. But I am the opposite of a stage magician. He gives you illusion that has the appearance of the truth. I give you truth in the pleasant disguise of illusion.

To begin with, I turn back time. I reverse it to that quaint period, the thirties, when the huge middle-class of America was matriculating in a school for the blind. Their eyes had failed them, or they had failed their eyes, and so they were having their fingers pressed forcibly down on the fiery Braille alphabet of a dissolving economy.

In Spain there was revolution. Here there was only shouting and confusion.

In Spain there was Guernica. Here there were disturbances of labour, sometimes pretty violent, in otherwise peaceful cities such as Chicago, Cleveland, Saint Louis . . .

This is the social background of the play.

Music.

The play is memory.

Being a memory play, it is dimly lighted. It is sentimental, it is not realistic.

In memory, everything seems to happen to music. That explains the fiddle in the wings.

I am the narrator of the play, and also a character in it.

The other characters are my mother, Amanda, my sister, Laura, and a gentleman caller who appears in the final scenes.

He is the most realistic character in the play, being an emissary from a world of reality that we were somehow set apart from.

But since I have a poet's weakness for symbols, I am using this character also as a symbol; he is the long delayed but always expected something that we live for.

There is a fifth character in the play who doesn't appear except in this larger-than-life-size photograph over the mantel.

This is the father who left us a long time ago.

He was a telephone man who fell in love with long distances; he gave up his job with the telephone company and skipped the light fantastic out of town . . .

The last we heard of him was a picture postcard from Mazatlan, on the Pacific coast of Mexico, containing a message of two words –

'Hello – good-bye!' and no address,

I think the rest of the play will explain itself . . .

The Glass Menagerie, Tennessee Williams (1945)

COMMENTARY   Arthur Miller's stage directions immediately suggest a non-naturalistic play in which things hold a symbolic, rather than a literal, meaning. The opening melody tells 'of grass and trees and the horizon', and 'an air of the [American] dream clings' to the Salesman's house. Set and lighting also have a symbolic effect: the 'towering, angular shapes' which surround the Salesman's house are threatening and perhaps represent the way in which (as we soon discover) the Salesman himself has become overwhelmed by a now hostile and competitive society. Lighting adds to this effect: blue light falls on the house, but 'the surrounding area shows an angry glow of orange.' Perhaps the most obvious non-naturalistic aspect is the fact that 'whenever the action is in the present the actors observe the imaginary wall-lines, entering the house only through the door at the left. But in the scenes of the past these boundaries are broken, and characters enter or leave a room by stepping 'through' a wall on to the forestage.' Rather than pretending to present only external reality, the set (and actors' interactions with it) suggests that in fact the play is *impressionistic* (see Chapter 2): we often see things as Willy Loman sees them.

Tennessee Williams' opening is equally striking in its departure from naturalism in its use, not just of a narrator (after all, we find these in Shakespeare), but one who is aware of his function as an '*undisguised convention of the play*' (to quote from Williams' opening stage directions). His references to the technicalities of stage business – 'In memory everything seems to happen to music. That explains the fiddle in the wings' – draw attention to this. This could be said to be *baring the device*, a technique recognised by Formalist criticism (see Chapter 5) in which conventions which would normally be taken for granted are exposed and emphasised. The play is also impressionistic – as Tom says, 'The play is memory'.

Both the Miller and Williams extracts demonstrate the way in which playwrights can deviate from naturalistic stage action to considerable effect, whether serious or comic. It is always worth being vigilant to moments when playwrights step away from the conventions of naturalism: it is usually a point with a considerable amount to say. In his 'Production Notes' to *The Glass Menagerie*, Williams wrote:

> Being a 'memory' play, The Glass Menagerie *can be presented with unusual freedom from convention. Because of its considerable delicate or tenuous material, atmospheric touches and subtleties of direction play a particularly important part. Expressionism and all other conventional techniques in drama have only one valid aim, and that is a closer approach to truth.*

ACTIVITY 41

Key skills: communication – reading/writing documents

You have now developed enough skills to approach drama texts in detail. Respond to the following extracts from different periods, working on your own.

1 Read the following extract from *The Duchess of Malfi* and, using the skills you have already developed for analysing dialogue, write a critical analysis of it focusing on the characters of the Duchess and Bosola as they appear in the scene. Consider:

- The importance of Bosola's asides
- The language each character uses and what it suggests about them
- The way in which the characters may move on the stage (how would you present the Duchess's obvious pregnancy or Bosola's asides?)
- To what extent Bosola could be considered a villainous 'type'.

(The Duchess of Malfi is secretly pregnant to her husband Antonio after marrying against the wishes of her brother, Ferdinand. Ferdinand has paid Bosola, a melancholy and wicked malcontent, to spy on the Duchess and find out her secret. He has procured some apricots to give to the Duchess, which were thought to induce labour.)

(Enter DUCHESS, OLD LADY, LADIES)
DUCHESS: Your arm Antonio, do I not grow fat?
I am exceeding short-winded. Bosola,
I would have you, sir, provide for me a litter,
Such a one, as the Duchess of Florence rode in.
BOSOLA: The duchess us'd one, when she was great with child.
DUCHESS: I think she did. Come hither, mend my ruff,
Here; when? Thou art such a tedious lady; and
Thy breath smells of lemon peels; would thou hadst done;
Shall I swound under your fingers? I am
So troubled with the mother.
BOSOLA: *(aside)*   I fear too much.
DUCHESS: I have heard you say that the French courtiers
Wear their hats on 'fore the king.
ANTONIO: I have seen it.
DUCHESS: In the presence.
ANTONIO: Yes.
DUCHESS: Why should we not bring up that fashion?
'Tis ceremony more than duty, that consists
In the removing of a piece of felt:
Be you the example to the rest o'th'court,
Put on your hat first.
ANTONIO: You must pardon me:
I have seen, in colder countries than in France,
Nobles stand bare to th' prince; and the distinction
Methought show'd reverently.
BOSOLA: I have a present for your Grace.
DUCHESS: For me, sir?
BOSOLA: Apricocks, Madam.
DUCHESS: O sir, where are they?
I have heard of none to-year.
BOSOLA: *(aside)* Good, her colour rises.
DUCHESS: Indeed I thank you: they are wondrous fair ones.
What an unskilful fellow is our gardener!
We shall have none this month.
BOSOLA: Will not your Grace pare them?
DUCHESS: No, they taste of musk, methinks; indeed they do.
BOSOLA: I know not: yet I wish your Grace had par'd 'em.
DUCHESS: I forgot to tell you the knave gard'ner,
Only to raise his profit by them the sooner,
Did ripen them in horse-dung.
BOSOLA: Oh, you jest.
DUCHESS: *(To Antonio)* You shall judge: pray taste one.
ANTONIO: Indeed, Madam,
I do not love the fruit.
DUCHESS: Sir, you are loth
To rob us of our dainties: 'tis a delicate fruit,
They say they are restorative?

BOSOLA: Tis a pretty art,
This *grafting*.
DUCHESS: 'Tis so: a bett'ring of nature.
BOSOLA: To make a pippin grow upon a crab,
A damson on a blackthorn: *(Aside)* How greedily
she eats them!
A whirlwind strike off these bawd *farthingales*,
For, but for that, and the loose-bodied gown,
I should have discover'd apparently
The young *springal* cutting a caper in her belly.

grafting: in gardening, the grafting
of one species onto another:
also, sexual intercourse.

farthingales: petticoats

springal: sapling

The Duchess of Malfi, John Webster, Act I, sc. ii, ll. 111–155, (1614)

2 The following extract is from a more recent
play, *Owners* by Caryl Churchill (1972).
Again, write a critical analysis. This time,
focus on the following:

■ The characters and the tempo, and how this
creates the mood

■ To what extent the extract is humorous. If
there is humour, how is it created?
■ How the theme of ownership is explored in
the extract.

*(Spurred by his wife's infidelity, Clegg the butcher is considering murdering her.
Worsely works for Clegg's wife dealing in property and is having an affair with her.
He is continually attempting suicide, but failing. In this extract, he is making Clegg a
cup of tea.)*

CLEGG: Weedkiller.
WORSELY: Sugar.
CLEGG: Two for me.
WORSELY: I wouldn't try to hang myself again.
CLEGG: Weedkiller in Marion's soup. In a garlic soup. Would it taste?
WORSELY: Try some and see.
CLEGG: I read of someone just got a splash in an orange drink and poured it away
when she tasted but even so that sip was fatal. It took a week mind you.
WORSELY: You'd have a job explaining.
CLEGG: I don't care. I don't care. I've had enough bottling up. Something must
explode.
WORSELY: My befriender the Samaritan believes life is God-given. At first he was too
sensitive to say so, but now in the interests of our befriendship he talks about his real
feelings. Life is leasehold. It belongs to God the almighty landlord. You mustn't take
your life because it's God's property not yours. I tell him if there's anything I own it's
what I stand up in.
CLEGG: That old suit?
WORSELY: My flesh and blood. The contraption I am in. The contraption I am.
CLEGG: It's not illegal now I'm glad to say. I couldn't have let Marion employ a
criminal.
WORSELY: Why was it illegal? The life as property of the state?
CLEGG: In the free world?
WORSELY: In wartime it is.
CLEGG: In wartime, naturally. No, I believe it was against the law because it was
wrong morally.
WORSELY: And now it no longer is?
CLEGG: Apparently not.
WORSELY: Though in any case the law's not for morals so much as property. The
legal system was made by owners. A man can do what he likes with his own.
CLEGG: Try telling Marion.
WORSELY: A house the same. Your own. You knock the door out if you like. That's

what it's for. A car the same. You drive how you like. Within a reasonable speed limit.
My flesh and blood the same.
CLEGG: A wife the same.
WORSELY: A wife is a person.
CLEGG: First and foremost a wife. One flesh. Marion leaves me.
WORSELY: She's basically fond.
CLEGG: Every morning she leaves me to go to work.
WORSELY: Work's a virtue.
CLEGG: And every evening she leaves me, leaves me, leaves me.
WORSELY: Goes out?
CLEGG: Or stays in. But not with me. Not being my wife. Not paying attention.

Owners, Caryl Churchill (1972)

Chapter review

In this chapter, you have looked in detail at a number of aspects of dramatic language and action, and the ways in which dramatists create specific effects. In reading a drama text, you can now:

- *analyse the way in which a dramatist creates an illusion of everyday, spontaneous speech, whether in monologue or dialogue;*
- *judge the tempo of dialogue, understand how it is created and the effect it has on the audience;*
- *consider the construction of a play and the way the playwright manipulates the audience's reactions for effect;*
- *understand how comedy is created in a piece of drama;*
- *respond to characters in dramatic texts, both as individual creations and dramatic constructions;*
- *appreciate the use of non-naturalistic conventions, and the use of symbolism through aspects of staging.*

4 Contexts for Drama Texts

You will now consider some of the contexts which can surround a literary work, and see the way in which they can affect individual texts in two case studies: Othello *by William Shakespeare, and* Doctor Faustus *by Christopher Marlowe.*

Putting context into context

No text exists in a vacuum. Any text, whether literary or non-literary, dramatic or non-dramatic, is produced in a given number of circumstances which can affect its production and reception. The title used above is probably how you have met the term in its everyday 'context': someone may excuse their bad behaviour by claiming it 'needs to be seen in a wider context'; or politicians may complain that their comments were 'taken out of context'. The literary meaning is similar, although more specific – the contexts of a text are the wider number of influencing factors we must consider before fully understanding a piece of literature. It is for this reason that Assessment Objective 5 states that you must **understand** the contexts of your text for study and also be able to **evaluate** their significance. This chapter will provide you with the skills to do that. The following activity will provide you with an awareness of what those influencing factors can be.

ACTIVITY 42

Key skills: communication – reading/discussion

1 Individually, spend some time reading the text below and decide exactly what you think it is about. There is no necessary right answer here – the text is such that it could have as many different meanings as readers (or audiences – an important aspect of texts that we will consider in the next chapter). The important aspect of this activity is the questions you ask about the text.

If you can, word-process the text yourself. If not, photocopy it. Jot down the questions that occur to you next to the text as you work through it. It may be that your ideas change as you read it.

2 Next, in groups, discuss the questions you asked as you looked for meanings in the text. Were your interpretations similar, or wildly different?

Request Stop

A queue at a Request Bus Stop. A WOMAN at the head, with a SMALL MAN in a raincoat next to her, two other WOMEN and a MAN.

WOMAN: *(to SMALL MAN)* I beg your pardon, what did you say?

Pause.

All I asked you was if I could get a bus from here to Shepherd's Bush.

Pause.

Nobody asked you to start making insinuations.

Pause.

Who do you think you are?

Pause.

Huh. I know your sort, I know your type. Don't worry, I know all about people like you.

Pause.

We can all tell where you come from. They're putting your sort inside every day of the week.

Pause.

All I've got to do, is report you, and you'd be standing in the dock in next to no time. One of my best friends is a plain clothes detective.

Pause.

I know all about it. Standing there as if butter wouldn't melt in your mouth. Meet you in a dark alley it'd be ... another story. *(To the others, who stare into space.)* You heard what this man said to me. All I asked him was if I could get a bus from here to Shepherd's Bush. *(To him.)* I've got witnesses, don't you worry about that.

Pause.

Impertinence.

Pause.

Ask a man a civil question he treats you like a threepenny bit. *(To him.)* I've got better things to do, my lad, I can assure you. I'm not going to stand here and be insulted on a public highway. Anyone can tell you're a foreigner. I was born just around the corner. Anyone can tell you're just up from the country for a bit of a lark. I know your sort.

Pause.

She goes to a LADY.

Excuse me lady. I'm thinking of taking this man up to the magistrate's court, you heard him make that crack, would you like to be a witness?

The LADY steps into the road.

LADY: Taxi ...

She disappears.

WOMAN: We know what sort she is. *(Back to position.)* I was the first in this queue.

Pause.

Born just round the corner. Born and bred. These people from the country haven't the faintest idea of how to behave. Peruvians. You're bloody lucky I don't put you on a charge. You ask a straightforward question –

The others suddenly thrust out their arms at a passing bus. They run off left after it. The WOMAN, alone, clicks her teeth and mutters. A MAN walks from the right to the stop, and waits. She looks at him out of the corner of her eye. At length she speaks shyly, hesitantly, with a slight smile.

Excuse me. Do you know if I can get a bus from here . . . to Marble Arch?

COMMENTARY

You may have asked all or some of the following questions as you worked through the extract:

- Is this the text in its entirety, or is it only a section of a longer piece?
- Had the man actually said something to the woman to provoke the outburst?
- Is it significant that the man is 'small', or that he is wearing a raincoat?
- Is the text a satire on feminism? Or is it a satire on prejudice, particularly xenophobia ('I know your sort . . . Anyone can tell you're a foreigner')?
- Where should this text be performed? In a theatre? Outdoors (possibly at a real bus stop)?
- What kind of text is it? The layout suggests a play – but what kind? A monologue? A comedy?
- When was the play written? You may have picked up on aspects of language which date it, such as 'threepenny bits'. Is the date important to our understanding of its meaning?
- What is the gender of the writer? Would this affect our understanding of the portrayal of the woman?
- Should the woman be seen to be disturbed? Does she appear outwardly respectable, or not? This may determine whether the play is seen as comic or not.

ACTIVITY 43

Key skills: communication – discussion

All of the above questions can be linked to different kinds of contexts for texts. In pairs, match up the questions asked about *Request Stop* with the following different contexts:

Textual: What we know about the text itself: whether it is complete, or an extract from a larger work.

Literary: The kind of writing it is. Does it have any recognisable features that will help us identify its genre and/or intention (i.e. to be comic or serious)? Does it remind us of anything else we have read?

Historical: When the play was written. The way it fits into a given time period.

Philosophical: Ideas we can recognise in the text that have a wider social meaning, for example, prejudice. This can also date the piece.

Biographical: Who the author is, and the way in which their biography sheds any light on the meaning of the text.

Linguistic: The language used. Is it specific to a particular period, or group of people?

COMMENTARY The clues you may have been looking for in your attempt to understand the text relate very clearly to the contexts you have just read. If you were wondering whether the text was complete or an extract, or if you were considering what type of text it was, then you were focusing on *textual* and *literary* contexts; if you were wondering when the play was written, or whether it was a satire on feminism, then you were dealing with *historical* or *philosophical* contexts. If you used the language to help you then you were using *linguistic* cues, and any consideration of the gender of the writer represents a very clear *biographical* context.

ACTIVITY 44

Key skills: communication – writing documents

Individually, continue *Request Stop* until it reaches a logical ending. Try to answer as many of the puzzling questions raised by the original text as you can. For example, you might give a reason for the woman's strange behaviour. When you have done it, compare versions with others in the class and, if time, perform the best ones.

Contexts for Writing and Performance

The set of contexts listed refers to the context of *writing*, but the same set of contexts exist for its *reception*. In other words, if you were watching a piece of Victorian drama, it may well be the attitudes you held were very different to those of audiences at the time of its first performance and this will no doubt affect your reaction to it.

Of course, as we discussed in Chapter 1, drama is particularly unique in that it can have a different context for every new performance. The play you looked at in the last activity – and it is a complete play, *Request Stop* by Harold Pinter, written in 1959 – would have a very different performance context if it was performed on a proscenium stage rather than, say, in the round. If the opening exchange were performed at a real bus stop, the effect could be striking to say the least!

ACTIVITY 45

Key skills: communication – discussion/presentation

In groups of six (or five for a smaller class), perform Pinter's *Request Stop*. Each group should perform the play with a different performance context. Choose one of the following:

– proscenium stage
– in the round
– on a street (if you dare!)
– with the woman as high class
– with the woman as a bag lady.

After you have watched the performances, discuss their different effects.

An interesting example of the multiple contextual contexts (sorry) that can surround drama is Arthur Miller's play *The Crucible*. This could be said to have three sets of contexts:

1 *The Crucible* is based on the real event of the Salem witch-hunts in Massachusetts in 1692, in which many innocent people were hanged.

This immediately provides a set of very different historical circumstances and beliefs which motivate the characters;

2. Miller wrote the play in the 1950s, intending it on one level as a covert attack on the mass hysteria created by the McCarthyite political persecutions of alleged communists. This context is clearly important in our understanding of the allegorical meaning of the play;

3. However, Miller himself made the point that the play's wider message should not have to relate specifically to McCarthyism. A recent writer compared the situation in the play with the recent spate of cases in America where children accused their parents of abuse. In this way, contexts which come after the text has been written can be as important as those which surrounded its creation.

ACTIVITY 46

Key skills: communication – discussion

Here are two lists: one of plays (some individual, and in some cases, by genre – see Chapter 2 if you need to jog your memory); and one of contextual events. As a whole class, discuss which contexts would affect our understanding of which plays and in what way. It may be that more than one context would affect any one play or genre of play. A commentary is at the end of the chapter.

List One

a The Holocaust and World War II
b 1960s liberation and rock n' roll
c Darwin's *Origin of Species* and evolutionary theory
d The European Union
e Recent events and attitudes to the Monarchy
f Suffragettes and the feminist movement

List Two

i Sophocles' *Antigone,* a tragedy where Antigone rebels against the decree of the tyrannical ruler of Thebes and gives the body of her traitor brother a decent burial;
ii Medieval mystery plays;
iii *Henry V,* a patriotic play about the Battle of Agincourt;
iv Restoration comedy and comedy of manners;
v *The Duchess of Malfi* by John Webster, in which the Duchess is murdered on her brother's command because she has shamed him because she married against his wishes;
vi *The Merchant of Venice,* about the cruel Jewish moneylender Shylock, who gets his just deserts.

WARNING!

Be aware of the distinction between different contexts and different interpretations (see Chapter 5). This is more difficult in drama than in poetry or prose, as in performance the two can exist together. A new interpretation of a play can also represent a new context for it!

Review

You have explored practically the ways different contexts affect our understanding of literature. These contexts can broadly be summed up as the following:

■ *textual* – how a section of a text can relate to the whole

- *intertextual* – how a text relates to other texts
- *linguistic* – how the language used relates to the period
- *biographical* – how a text relates to the life of the writer
- *intellectual* – how a text relates to social, political or religious ideas
- *historical* – self-explanatory (although bear in mind the comments of New Historicists in Chapter 5).

Fairly obviously, not all contexts are of relevance to all plays and some contexts play a more important role than others in our understanding of them.

It is probably fair to say that we have to work harder to understand the contexts of plays the older they are, for the simple reason that the set of beliefs, attitudes, living conditions and conventions are more alien to us. You are now going to look at contexts in action in two complete plays from the Renaissance period (1550–1660): William Shakespeare's *Othello* (1603) and Christopher Marlowe's *Doctor Faustus* (1592). You may or may not be studying these texts at AS or A Level (both are frequently set texts). Even if you are not, they will give you a clear understanding of how texts relate to their contexts and how to deal with them.

ACTIVITY 47

Key Skills: information technology – different sources

Find as much information as you can on the Renaissance period in England from CD-ROM or the Internet, using the addresses given in the Further Reading section, or any others of use.

Focus on the following areas which will prove a useful supplement to the contexts provided:

- monarchy
- religion
- society
- important historical events.

'Haply, for I am black …' Case Study 1: *Othello, The Moor of Venice*

ACTIVITY 48

Key skills: communication – reading/ discussion

1 If you are not studying *Othello*, familiarise yourself with the plot, preferably through reading the play or watching a performance of it (there are some excellent televised versions). If time is short, find a brief summary of the play.

2 On page 77 is a still from a production of *Othello* at the Savoy Theatre in 1930, with Paul Robeson as Othello and Peggy Ashcroft as Desdemona. In groups, discuss your initial reactions to the photograph. What contexts do you think are apparent in it? How much is this to do with the date of the production?

ACTIVITY 49

**Key skills: communication –
reading/presentation**

The following extracts all represent different
contexts for *Othello*.

1 Individually: read the context extracts and
   decide what kind of context they are, from
   the list you created on page 71. Make sure
   you understand them and write down your
   ideas as to what information they reveal and
   how they may relate to *Othello*.

2 In pairs: each pair take one of the extracts
   from *Othello*, act it out and then:
   i   identify lines from the contextual material
   and the extract which deal with similar
   themes and write them out next to each
   other on a separate piece of paper

   ii discuss exactly what the links are between
   the contextual material and your extract,
   and then evaluate their significance. How
   large a part do the attitudes and ideas
   expressed have in the play? Does the
   action in the extracts agree with the
   contextual material, or contradict it?

3 Feed back your ideas on your extracts to the
   class and reach a class decision as to the
   relationship between the contexts and the
   play.

Context Extract 1

Alas, alas, and *wele-wo*!   *wele-wo*: expression of sorrow
Lucifer, why fell thou so?
We, that were angels so fair,
And sat so high above the air,
Now are we *waxen* black as any coal,   *waxen*: grown
And ugly, tattered as a foal.

(*The Creation*, in *The Towneley Plays*)

Context Extract 2

Whereas the Queen's majesty, tendering the good welfare of her own natural
subjects, greatly distressed in these hard times of dearth, is highly discontented to
understand the great numbers of Negroes and blackamoors which (as she is
informed) are crept into this realm since the troubles between her highness and the
King of Spain; who are fostered and relieved here, to the great annoyance of her own

liege people who want the relief which these people consume, as also for that most of them are infidels having no understanding of Christ or his Gospel: hath given especial commandment that the said kind of people shall be with all speed avoided and discharged out of this her majesty's dominion; and to that end and purpose hath appointed Caspar van Senden, merchant of Lubcheck, for their speedy transportation, a man that hath very well deserved of this realm respect that by his own labour and charge he hath relieved and brought from Spain diverse of our English nation, who otherwise would have perished there. These shall therefore be to will and assist you and every of you to aid and assist the said Caspar van Senden, or his associates to take up such Negroes and blackamoors to be transported as aforesaid, as he shall find realm within the realm of England; and if there shall be any persons or persons which are possessed of such blackamoors that refuse to deliver them in sort as aforesaid, then we require you to call them before you and to advise and persuade them by all good means to satisfy her majesty's pleasure therein ...

(Elizabeth I, 1601)

Context Extract 3

It manifestly and plainely appeareth by Holy Scripture, that after the general inundation and overflowing of the earth, there remained no more men alive but Noe and his three sonnes, Sem, Cham, and Japhet, who onely were left to possess and inhabite the whole face of the earth ... he straitely commanded his sonnes and their wives, that they should with reverence and fear beholde the justice and mighty power of God, and that during the time of the floud while they remained in the Arke, they should use continencie, and abstaine from carnall copulation with their wives ... which good instructions and exhortations notwithstanding his wicked sonne Cham disobeyed, and being perswaded that the first childe borne after the flood (by right and Lawe of nature) should inherite and possesse all the dominions of the earth, hee contrary to his fathers commandement while they were yet in the Arke, used company with his wife, and craftily went about thereby to dis-inherite the offspring of his other two brethren: for the which wicked and detestable fact, as an example for contempt for Almightie God, and disobedience of parents, God would a sonne should bee borne whose name was Chus, who not onely itself, but all his posteritie after him should bee so blacke and lothsome, that it might remain a spectacle of disobedience to all the world. And of this blacke and cursed Chus came all these black Moores which are in Africa.

(*Discourse* from Richard Hakluyt's *Voyages*)

Context Extract 4

(*Tamora, Queen of the Goths, has just given birth – and the baby is clearly the product of her affair with Aaron, the Moor.*)

NURSE: O, that which I would hide from heaven's eye,
Our empress' shame, and stately Rome's disgrace.
She is delivered, lords, she is delivered.
AARON: To whom?
NURSE: I mean she is brought abed.
AARON: Well, God give her rest! What hath he sent her?
NURSE: A devil.
AARON: Why, then she is the devil's dam: a joyful issue.
NURSE: A joyless, dismal, black and sorrowful issue.
Here is the babe, as loathsome as a toad
Amongst the fair fac'd breeders of our clime;
The empress sends it thee, thy stamp, thy seal,
And bids thee christen it with a dagger's point.
AARON: Zounds, ye whore! Is black so base a hue?

Sweet *blowse*, ye are a beauteous blossom, sure.   *blowse*: wench
DEMETRIUS: Villain, what hast thou done?
AARON: That which thou canst not undo.
CHIRON: Thou hast undone our mother.
AARON: Villain, I have done thy mother.
DEMETRIUS: And therein, hellish dog, thou hast undone her.
Woe to her chance, and damn'd her loathed choice!
Accurs'd the offspring of so foul a fiend!

Titus Andronicus, Shakespeare (1594)

Context Extract 5

WHITE ANGER SPILLS OVER IN AFTERMATH OF OJ ACQUITTAL

By Tim Cornwell in Los Angeles

The talk radio shows in Los Angeles still rang with white anger over the OJ Simpson verdict yesterday. At Nicole Brown Simpson's townhouse, a printed sign read 'OJ Must Die.' Nearby a lone woman protested with a placard that read: 'OJ Simpson, wife beater, wife killer.'

Five days after the former football hero was acquitted by a black-dominated jury of the double murder of his white ex-wife and her friend Ronald Goldman, race still intrudes at every turn, from virtual shouting matches in television show audiences to the letters pages of the *Los Angeles Times*. In an interview with the newspaper *USA Today*, President Bill Clinton called on people not to use the 'polarisation of perception' on the case to widen the gap between black and white. It would be a great mistake if 'this became the beginning of some new division in our country,' he said.

The Independent, 7.10.95

Othello: Extract 1

BRABANTIO: O thou foul thief, where hast thou stowed my daughter?
Damned as thou art, thou hast enchanted her,
For I'll refer me to all things of sense,
If she in chains of magic were not bound,
Whether a maid so tender, fair and happy,
So opposite to marriage that she shunned
The wealthy, curled darlings of our nation,
Would ever have, t'incur a general mock,
Run from her guardage to the sooty bosom
Of such a thing as thou? To fear, not to delight.
Judge me the world if 'tis not gross in sense
That thou hast practised on her with foul charms,
Abus'd her delicate youth with drugs or minerals
That weakens motion: I'll have't disputed on,
'Tis probable and palpable to thinking.
I therefore apprehend and do attach thee
For an abuser of the world, a practiser
Of arts inhibited and out of warrant.
Lay hold upon him; if he do resist
Subdue him at his peril!

Othello, Act I, sc. ii, ll. 62–81

Othello: Extract 2

IAGO: My lord, I see you're moved.
OTHELLO: No, not much moved.
I do not think but Desdemona's honest.
IAGO: Long live she so: and long live you to think so.

OTHELLO: And yet how nature, erring from itself –
IAGO: Ay, there's the point: as, to be bold with you,
Not to affect many proposed matches
Of her own clime, complexion and degree,
Whereto we see, in all things, nature tends –
Foh! One may smell in such a will most rank,
Foul disproportion, thoughts unnatural.
But pardon me, I do not in position
Distinctly speak of her, though I may fear
Her will, recoiling to her better judgement,
May fall to match you with her country forms,
And happily repent.

Othello, Act III, sc. iii, ll. 227–242

Othello: Extract 3

OTHELLO: This fellow's of exceeding honesty
And knows all qualities, with a learned spirit
Of human dealings. If I do prove her *haggard*,   *haggard*: an untamed hawk
Though that her *jesses* were my dear heart-strings,   *jesses*: straps
I'd whistle her off and let her down the wind
To prey at fortune. Haply for I am black
And have not these soft parts of conversation
That chamberers have, or for I am declined
Into the vale of years – yet that's not much –
She's gone, I am abused, and my relief
Must be to loathe her. O curse of marriage
That we can call these delicate creatures ours
And not their appetites! I had rather be a toad
And live upon the vapour of a dungeon
Than keep a corner in the thing I love
For others' uses.

Othello, Act III, sc. iii, ll. 262–277

Othello: Extract 4

OTHELLO: Why, how should she be murdered?
EMILIA: Alas, who knows?
OTHELLO: You heard her say yourself it was not I.
EMILIA: She said so: I must needs report the truth.
OTHELLO: She's like a liar gone to burning hell:
'Twas I that killed her.
EMILIA: O, the more angel she,
And you the blacker devil!
OTHELLO: She turned to folly, and she was a whore.
EMILIA: Thou dost belie her, and thou art a devil.
OTHELLO: She was as false as water.
EMILIA: Thou art as rash as fire to say
That she was false. O, she was heavenly true!
OTHELLO: Cassio did top her: ask thy husband else.
O, I were damned beneath all depth in hell
But that I did proceed upon just grounds
To this extremity. Thy husband knew it well.
EMILIA: My husband?
OTHELLO: Thy husband.
EMILIA: That she was false?
To wedlock?

OTHELLO: Ay, with Cassio. Had she been true,
If heaven would make me such another world
Of one entire and perfect *chrysolite*,   *chrysolite*: a precious stone
I'd not have sold her for it.
EMILIA: My husband?
OTHELLO: Ay, 'twas he that told me on her first;
An honest man he is, and hates the slime
That sticks on filthy deeds.
EMILIA: My husband!
OTHELLO: What needs
This iterance, woman? I say thy husband.
EMILIA: O mistress, villainy hath made mocks with love!
My husband say she was false?
OTHELLO: He, woman;
I say thy husband: dost understand the word?
My friend thy husband, honest, honest Iago.
EMILIA: If he say so, may his pernicious soul
Rot half a grain a day! He lies to th' heart:
She was too fond of her most filthy bargain!
OTHELLO: Ha!
EMILIA: Do thy worst:
This deed of thine is no more worthy heaven
Than thou wast worthy her.

Othello, Act V, sc. ii, ll. 123–157

COMMENTARY The contextual extracts clearly deal with racist views of blackness. Extracts 1 and 3 demonstrate Elizabethan religious explanations for black skin colour; both relate blackness to sin, whether it is the sin of the 'angels' who fell with Satan from heaven, or the children of Cham, who 'remain a spectacle of disobedience to all the world.' Cham also represents another aspect of Elizabethan views of Africans – their 'carnality'. Explorers' reports of the time constantly presented a *discourse* (see page 107) of Africans as sexually voracious and promiscuous, making much of their multiple wives: Cham, unable to resist having sex with his wife, represents this belief.

This stereotype can also be seen clearly in the character of Aaron the Moor from Shakespeare's *Titus Andronicus*, who has slept with and impregnated, Tamora, something he crudely boasts about – 'Villain, I have done your mother.' This text is very useful in our understanding of *Othello*, as it shows Shakespeare's attitude to Moors elsewhere – other works by a writer can form a useful context. In this case, Aaron is without doubt a villain – cruel, deceitful and lecherous – although he could almost be representing his race when he cries 'Is black so base a hue?'

Elizabeth's proclamation has a more practical purpose, dealing with the large number of 'Negroes and blackamoors' which have 'crept' into the realm, 'who are fostered and relieved here, to the great annoyance of her own liege people who want the relief which these people consume' (an argument we could expect to hear today from a character such as Alf Garnett). Interestingly, the proclamation also suggests that a number of people in England were 'possessed of such blackamoors', no doubt as servants, which probably means that Shakespeare had some everyday experience of at least seeing, if not conversing with, people of African background. This might have given him a more sensitive insight into their characters than the exotic and exaggerated travellers' reports of the time.

If we now turn to the extracts from *Othello*, evidence of racism is clearly apparent: Brabantio considers him a 'foul thief' and can only assume he has 'enchanted' his daughter for her to choose 'the sooty bosom/Of such a thing as thou'; and Emilia throws considerable racial abuse at him, calling him 'a devil' and 'her most filthy bargain.' Iago plays on race in his so-called 'temptation' of Othello, actually using Desdemona's love for Othello as evidence of her 'thoughts unnatural'. If she can fall in love with a black man, his logic goes, then she could do anything. Notice that Othello agrees with such an idea and in fact suggests it: 'And yet how nature, erring in itself'. In Extract 3 he even says 'Haply, for I am black . . .' in his consideration of her alleged faithlessness! Othello could be said to have *internalised* the racism he has experienced.

The important question is, of course, whether Shakespeare's presentation of Othello agrees with, or contradicts, the racist views which clearly existed. New Historicist critics (see next chapter) claim that literature can either be part of the *dominant* culture (that is, it follows the attitudes and beliefs of the time) or it can be part of a *subordinate* culture which contradicts them. Which Shakespeare is doing isn't an easy question to answer and depends to a large extent on an individual's interpretation. One of the aspects of the Paul Robeson/Peggy Ashcroft production you may have picked up on is the clear vulnerability of Desdemona in front of Othello and his sheer physical presence, most startling in the hand around her throat, which also shows the contrast between their skin colours. But what is the hand doing? Is it threatening? Or, is it a caress? Even in a still photograph, some ambiguity can exist.

What we can say is that *Othello*'s genre is tragedy and that by definition Othello is a tragic hero. He experiences emotions on a grand scale and is capable of great nobility, passion and beautiful poetry. He is a victim of Iago's plotting just as Desdemona is and, in many ways, is also a victim of the racist views of the time. His internalised racism – that is, his own belief that Desdemona could not love him because he is black – is one of the main factors in his jealousy. In this way, Shakespeare could be seen to be criticising the racist beliefs at the time. However, he could also be seen as *pandering* to the racist views of the time, presenting his audience with a violent, emotional black man who goes mad, rolls his eyes and ultimately murders his innocent (and very white) wife.

It is here that the final context – the OJ Simpson story – fits in. As you discovered earlier, the contexts of a text's *re*ception can be as important as those of its *in*ception; and in the OJ Simpson case there is a clear parallel with the story of Othello. The story focuses on the racist aspects of the case. There is 'white fury' at the decision by a 'black-dominated' jury to acquit the 'former football star' (suggesting racial bias, perhaps) for the 'double murder of his *white* ex-wife'. As the journalist points out, 'race intrudes at every turn'. Even in today's apparently prejudice-free world, the story of a black man murdering a white woman can stir powerful emotions.

Key skills: information technology – research

Use CD-ROM or the Internet to investigate other contexts to *Othello* such as:

- the role of women in society
- warfare
- the significance of Venice.

Key skills: communication – writing documents

Written assignment:
To what extent do you think Shakespeare's portrayal of Othello agrees with Elizabethan views of blackness?

Case Study 2: *The Tragical History of the Life and Death of Doctor Faustus*

We will now take a different dramatic text from slightly earlier in the Renaissance period – Christopher Marlowe's *Doctor Faustus*, written in c. 1592 – and briefly consider a number of different possible contexts for that play. Again, you will need to familiarise yourself with the story of Faustus to fully appreciate the activities. The play is shorter than *Othello* and contains a large number of scenes which have little relevance to the main plot, and so a 'condensed' reading shouldn't take too long. The extracts in this book are taken from an edition of the play based on the B text.

Different contexts for Dr Faustus

We will now look at the following contexts for *Doctor Faustus:*

- literary
- social
- philosophical
- biographical
- textual.

Literary context: Faustus and medieval drama

An important context for a literary work is the way in which it fits into a tradition. Clearly, when a literary text is produced, it is often the product of the influence of any number of previous works, even if the writer is not consciously aware of them. Styles, trends and forms already exist and the way in which a particular text fits into them is an important consideration. Sometimes writers will deliberately relate to, or refer to, earlier texts or traditions so that they come to form a part of the text's meaning. This is known as *intertextuality*. As an example, Tom Stoppard's play *Rosencrantz and Guildenstern are Dead* (1967) supposedly takes place in the wings of a performance of *Hamlet*, Rosencrantz and Guildenstern being two characters from Shakespeare's play. Tom Stoppard's play actually includes scenes from the original *Hamlet*. It is clear here that the meaning of this particular play relies heavily on another, even if we do not necessarily have to know the other play.

This kind of intertextuality is obvious, deliberate and extreme, but texts can influence other texts in more subtle and unconscious ways. Drama particularly often involves such literary contexts as there are many theatrical conventions available to a writer at a specific time and in a specific period. For example, *genre* was an important consideration for an Elizabethan dramatist. That being the case, any Elizabethan tragedy (or any tragedy, in fact) has as a context – the conventions and 'rules' of tragedy as they had appeared in earlier plays (see page 26). However, the set of conventions an Elizabethan dramatist had at their disposal would be very different from those of a modern playwright – the idea of writing a play wholly in prose, for example, would have seemed alien and untheatrical to them.

As Marlowe was one of the first major Elizabethan playwrights, when he wrote *Doctor Faustus* some of his main literary predecessors were those dramatists who had produced the Mystery and Morality Plays in the fifteenth and early sixteenth centuries. These therefore represent an important literary context to *Faustus*. That said, there were other tragedies written before *Faustus* that had already moved away from the traditions of medieval drama. To what extent Marlowe's play is a Morality Play has been a topic of considerable debate. Now it is your turn to decide!

ACTIVITY 51

Key skills: communication – reading/discussion

Re-read the description of the Medieval Mystery and Morality Plays in Chapter 2, and then look at the following two extracts from *Doctor Faustus*. In groups, discuss:

1 From the the extracts below, can the play be said to have a 'moral'?
2 Could the character of Faustus be said to represent a specific 'sin'? If so, what is it? Or is this too simplistic a view of his character?
3 What other aspects of medieval drama can you discover, either in the extracts below, or (if you know the play) in *Doctor Faustus* as a whole? Consider staging as well as just the words themselves.
4 Do you think that Marlowe was deliberately 'conjuring' the form of the Morality Play? How would this affect the play's meaning?

Doctor Faustus: Extract 1

FAUSTUS: Now, Faustus, must
Thou needs be damn'd, and canst thou not be sav'd.
What boots it then to think on God or heaven?
Away with such vain fancies, and despair;
Despair in God, and trust in Beelzebub.
Now go not backward; no, Faustus, be resolute:
Why waver'st thou? O, something soundeth in mine ears.
'Abjure this magic, turn to God again!'
Ay, and Faustus will turn to God again.
To God? He loves thee not:
The god thou serv'st is thine own appetite,
Wherein is fix'd the love of Beelzebub:
To him I'll build an altar and a church
And offer lukewarm blood of new-born babes.

Enter the two Angels.

BAD ANGEL: Go forward, Faustus, in that famous art.
GOOD ANGEL: Sweet Faustus, leave that execrable art.
FAUSTUS: Contrition, prayer, repentance, what of these?
GOOD ANGEL: O, they are means to bring thee unto heaven.
BAD ANGEL: Rather illusions, fruits of lunacy,
That make men foolish that do use them most.
GOOD ANGEL: Sweet Faustus, think of heaven and heavenly things.
BAD ANGEL: No, Faustus, think of honour and of wealth.

Exeunt Angels.

FAUSTUS: Wealth!
Why, the *signory of Emden* shall be mine.   *signory of Emden*: fleet of ships
When Mephostophilis shall stand by me,
What power can hurt me? Faustus, thou art safe:
Cast no more doubts! Mephostophilis, come,
And bring glad tidings from great Lucifer.
Is't not midnight? Come, Mephostophilis,
Veni, veni, Mephostophilis!
                                                    Come, come Mephostophilis!

                                                    Doctor Faustus, sc. v, ll. 1–30

Doctor Faustus: Extract 2

Enter the GOOD ANGEL and the BAD ANGEL at several doors.
GOOD ANGEL: O Faustus, if thou hadst given ear to me,
Innumerable joys had follow'd thee:
But thou didst love the world.
BAD ANGEL: Gave ear to me,
And now must taste Hell's pains perpetually.
GOOD ANGEL: O, what will all thy riches, pleasures, pomps
Avail thee now?
BAD ANGEL: Nothing but vex thee more,
To want in Hell, that had on earth much store.

Music while the throne descends.

GOOD ANGEL: O, thou hast lost celestial happiness,
Pleasures unspeakable, bliss without end.
Hadst thou affected sweet divinity,
Hell or the devil had had no power on thee.
Hadst thou kept on that way, Faustus, behold
In what resplendent glory thou hadst sit
In yonder throne, like those bright shining saints,
And triumph'd over hell: that hast thou lost.
And now, poor soul, must thy good angel leave thee;
The jaws of hell are open to receive thee.

Hell is discovered.

BAD ANGEL: Now, Faustus, let thine eyes with horror stare
Into that vast perpetual torture-house.
There are the furies, tossing damned souls
On burning forks; their bodies boil in lead:
There are live quarters broiling on the coals,
That ne'er can die: this ever-burning chair
Is for o'er-tortur'd souls to rest them in:
These that are fed with sops of flaming fire

Were gluttons and lov'd only delicates
And laugh'd to see the poor starve at their gates.
But yet all these are nothing; thou shalt see
Ten thousand tortures that more horrid be.
FAUSTUS: O, I have seen enough to torture me.
BAD ANGEL: Nay, thou must feel them, taste the smart of all:
He that loves pleasure must for pleasure fall:
And so I leave thee, Faustus, till anon;
Then wilt thou tumble in confusion.
Exit.

Doctor Faustus, sc. xix, ll. 99–132

ACTIVITY 52

Key skills: communication – discussion

Individually, read the following three 'resource documents':
Social Context: The Church in the Renaissance
Philosophical Context: The Supernatural in the Renaissance
Biographical Context: Christopher Marlowe, Playwright and Suspected Spy

Then, in groups discuss the following issues surrounding these religious, philosophical and biographical contexts:

1 How important to an understanding of

Doctor Faustus is the contextual information you have been given? Of the three, which context is the most important and why?

2 Do any of the contexts contradict or undermine each other? (For example, how might what Richard Baines says about Marlowe affect our consideration of the belief in the supernatural?)

3 How reliable do you consider the testimony of Thomas Kyd to be (think about the circumstances under which Kyd made his allegations)?

Social Context: The Church in the Renaissance

One of the major incidents of the Renaissance period was the Reformation, in which Henry VIII broke away from the Catholic Church and the control of the Pope in Rome, to set up the Church of England in 1533 – largely so that he could divorce his first wife Katharine of Aragon, something the Catholic Church refused to allow. Henry declared himself Head of the Church and dissolved the Catholic monasteries, which he considered to be a drain of public resources. However, under Henry the Church of England remained Catholic in its outlook. It was not until he died and his young son Edward inherited the throne that the Church became Protestant which, as the name suggests, implies a protest against the doctrines of the Catholic Church.

Protestantism rejected the Catholic Faith's emphasis on the central importance of the Mass and instead placed an emphasis on the individual's ability to find salvation through silent prayer and reading of the Bible. Texts such as Thomas Cranmer's *Book of Common Prayer* and new translations of the Bible encouraged this. Protestantism, greatly influenced by the French religious reformer Calvin, also rejected the pomp and display of the Catholic faith and instead focused on the more austere aspects of worship. Calvinism also emphasised the idea of original sin and pre-destination (or fate), as well as a belief in the literal existence of Hell and the Devil.

During Edward's short reign (1547–1553) Catholics were persecuted. As a reaction against this, on his death the throne was seized by Henry's eldest daughter Mary I, who briefly restored Catholicism and whose energetic persecution of Protestants led her to be known as 'Bloody Mary'. It was not until Elizabeth I took the throne in 1558 that the Church of England was re-established and still remains today. Although Protestant, the new Queen created what has been called the 'Elizabethan Settlement', which allowed both Protestants and Catholics to worship under the Church of England without feeling they had betrayed their 'true' faith. However, religious stability was still not absolute – the Church of England was excommunicated by the Pope in 1571 and the Puritans (extreme Protestants) continued to reject any aspect of the Catholic faith.

Philosophical Context: **The Supernatural in the Renaissance**

It is generally accepted that there was widespread belief in the occult during the fifteenth and sixteenth centuries. Rather than being seen simply as 'spooky' stories, witches, devils and spirits were seen as an existing threat. The Protestant religion, and in particular the theories of Calvin, taught that Hell was a very real place indeed and that the devil existed in a physical form with a legion of demons as followers.

The theatre also emphasised such a belief. Medieval Mystery Plays portrayed Satan as a human-like character and one side of the acting area represented (often very realistically) the mouth of Hell, fiery and gaping – a visible reminder to an audience of the existence of the Devil and his demons. Therefore, it was thought to be possible that, if allowed or 'conjured', he could find his way to earth in his search for more souls. In 1563, an Act was passed giving death as the penalty to any who 'use, practice or exercise invocations or conjurations of evil and wicked spirits to or for any evil intent and purpose,' and in 1602, the jury in a witchcraft case were told, 'The land is full of witches, they abound in all places.'

When James I took over the throne in 1603, he continued the persecution of so-called 'witches' with even more zest, often attending the torture of suspected witches himself. He had already written his own thesis on the subject, *Demonology*, before becoming King and, once King, he replaced the 1563 Act with a new Statute entitled 'Against Conjuration, Witchcraft, and Dealing with Evil and Wicked Spirits', giving even harsher penalties to those suspected of witchcraft. Interestingly, James wrote *Demonology*, he says, to contradict 'the damnable opinions of two principally in an age, whereof the one called SCOT an Englishman, is not ashamed in publike print to deny that there can be such a thing as witchcraft . . .'

The SCOT is Reginald Scot, an Englishman, who in 1584 published a work titled *The Discoverie Of Witchcraft*. As James's reference makes clear, this was a work which rejects Elizabethan views of witchcraft: the contents summary of Chapter 1 of Book V, for example, is 'Of transformations, ridiculous examples brought by the adversaries for the confirmation of their foolish doctrine.' Clearly, not everyone believed whole-heartedly in the doctrine of witchcraft and demonolatry: there were some dissenting voices.

Biographical Context: Christopher Marlowe, Playwright and Suspected Spy

Only a small amount is known about Christopher Marlowe, although what we do know makes him one of the most interestingly shady playwrights in English Literature! He was born in 1564, into a relatively humble background (his father was a cobbler). Nevertheless, because he clearly had talent from an early age, he won a scholarship to Corpus Christi College, Cambridge, probably with the intention of taking holy orders. However, from Cambridge he went straight into playwrighting, and wrote the very successful *Tamburlaine 1* and *2* the year he left. A problem arose with his degree when Cambridge said they would refuse to award it because he had not spent enough time in residence at the University; but interestingly, it was the Queen's own Council who stepped in to defend him. They claimed he had been working for the Queen – possibly in espionage. He has been linked with such 'spying' for the remainder of his life; he was called before the Queen's Council again the week before he died.

Marlowe's theatrical career was short-lived but explosively successful. He wrote *Doctor Faustus, The Jew of Malta, Dido Queen of Carthage* and *Edward II* (although not necessarily in that order – there has been some debate about when they were written), as well as some poetic works, all with great success. At one point, he had more fame and respect than Shakespeare himself.

That Marlowe was a 'lively' character can be seen from the fact that he was bound over to keep the peace in 1592, but it is his death that has stimulated people's imaginations. For example, Anthony Burgess recently provided a fictional account in his novel *A Dead Man in Deptford.* Marlowe died in the equivalent of a 'bar-room brawl' when he was stabbed in the eye in an argument with another man over the bill! However, some scholars have even suggested that there was more to it than that. When Marlowe was killed, a warrant was out for his arrest. This was because some papers had been found in the room of the playwright Thomas Kyd (see Chapter 2) making blasphemous allegations. In fear of torture and death,

Kyd had denied they were his and had claimed they were Marlowe's. He also made various other allegations about Marlowe's behaviour and 'monstrous opiniouns' regarding religion, such as 'things esteemed to be donn by devine power might have as well been donn by observation of men'; he was also 'intemperate & of a cruel hart' and 'wold sodenlie take slyght occasion to slyp out ... attempting sodden pryvie injuries to men'! Two days after Marlowe's death, a document was also given to the authorities by a man called Richard Baines, entitled 'A note containing the opinion of one Christopher Marly concerning his damnable Judgment of Religion, and scorn of God's word', containing such allegations as:

... almost into every company he cometh he persuades men to Atheism, willing them not to be afeard of bugbears and hobgoblins, and utterly scorning both God and his ministers as I Richard Baines will justify and approve both by mine own oath and the testimony of many honest men ...

ACTIVITY 53

Key skills: communication – discussion/writing documents

1 Individually, read and then take notes comparing the following extract from the play with the contextual information you have just read. What aspects of the scene relate directly to the contexts?

2 In pairs, compare your ideas and add to your notes.

3 Produce a written analysis of the scene, explaining its relationship to the social, philosophical and literary context.

MEPHOSTOPHILIS: Speak, Faustus, do you deliver this as your deed?
FAUSTUS: Ay, take it, and the devil give thee good on't!
MEPHOSTOPHILIS: Now, Faustus, ask what thou wilt.
FAUSTUS: First will I question with thee about hell.
Tell me, where is the place that men call hell?
MEPHOSTOPHILIS: Under the heavens.
FAUSTUS: Ay, so are all things else; but whereabouts?
MEPHOSTOPHILIS: Within the bowels of these elements,
Where we are tortured and remain forever.
Hell hath no limits, nor is circumscrib'd
In one self place, but where we are is hell,
And where hell is, there must we ever be;
And, to be short, when all the world dissolves
And every creature shall be purify'd,
All places shall be hell that is not heaven.
FAUSTUS: I think hell's a fable.
MEPHOSTOPHILIS: Ay, think so still, till experience change thy mind.
FAUSTUS: Why, dost thou think that Faustus shall be damn'd?
MEPHOSTOPHILIS: Ay, of necessity, for here's the scroll
In which thou hast given thy soul to Lucifer.
FAUSTUS: Ay, and body too; but what of that?
Think'st thou that Faustus is so fond to imagine
That after this life there is any pain?
No, these are trifles and mere old wives' tales.
MEPHOSTOPHILIS: But I am an instance to prove the contrary,
For I tell thee I am damn'd and now in hell.
FAUSTUS: Nay, and this be hell, I'll willingly be damn'd:
What, sleeping, eating, walking, and disputing!

Doctor Faustus, sc. v, ll. 113–140

Textual Contexts – or, when is a set text not a set text?

One of the contexts most often overlooked – a case of not seeing the wood for the trees, perhaps – is that of the very text itself. At its most basic, this refers to the way in which one part of a text fits into the whole. For example, we may judge a character's actions in relation to their behaviour in other parts of the play. However, particularly with older plays, often the 'textual' context means far more than this. *Doctor Faustus* is an excellent example of this.

Today when we read a text, we take it for granted that it is 'authoritative'. That is, it is the text the author intended us to read, give or take minor alterations by editors, say. This is due to the technological advances in text production in the twentieth century, where the same text can be produced millions of times in an identical form. Of course, in the Renaissance, this was far from the case. Textual production was a lengthy, inaccurate and expensive business and was unreliable for a number of reasons:

- Scribes would handwrite the text, often based on patchy notes and usually when the playwrights were dead, so there was no way of checking if the version was correct (playwrights were reluctant to let their manuscripts go as there were no 'copyright' laws to protect their work from being stolen).
- Touring acting companies were very irreverent in their use of texts, often cutting or changing them extensively to suit their tastes, audience and resources. There was none of the worship of the 'original text' that exists today.
- As a result, often when texts were finally written down by scribes, they were a mish-mash of the original text and other, later amendments.
- Even if the text itself was generally free from tampering, mistakes were often made in the copying because of poor handwriting and spelling (go on the Internet and look at some of Shakespeare's original manuscripts and take comfort if you are a poor speller!).

A large number of plays survived in what we think is a pretty close version of the original. However, some disappeared altogether and some exist in a mangled or problematic form. It is this last group to which *Doctor Faustus* belongs.

To put it simply, there are two existing texts of *Faustus,* the A and B text. The A text is shorter and earlier (from 1604). The B text contains a larger number of scenes and is from 1616. As both manuscripts were written after Marlowe's death, we do not know which was closer to the original and scholars have disagreed as to which is the 'best' text – in other words, closest to what Marlowe originally intended.

At one stage, it was generally accepted that the A text was better, as it was earlier (and therefore had more chance of being close to the original). Scholars also thought the extra scenes in the B text were inferior and were probably added by another, lesser playwright. However, then fashions changed. This time it was considered that the A text was probably a shortened, touring version of the play which had been cut by an acting company and that the B text was the real, full version of the original play. The A text has recently come back into favour – and still they argue on. It is one of the best examples of the fact that reading is an active process: texts are created, but then are recreated depending on the most influential readers, usually editors, who have to produce a text by choosing what they consider to be the best of 'variant readings' (differences in texts of the same play). If you are studying *Doctor Faustus*, then which text has been chosen by the editor? As the extracts in this book are all from the B text, it may be that you didn't recognise all of them. It may be that your concept of what constitutes the play *Doctor Faustus* is different from somebody else studying a different syllabus. Dizzying, isn't it?

ACTIVITY 54

Key skills: communication – research/reading

1 Compare the two different texts of *Doctor Faustus* (the New Mermaid edition is based on the A text, but gives as its appendix all the extra scenes in the B text). Do you think the extra scenes are inferior? Which text do you prefer?

Key skills: information technology – research/reading

2 Either use one of the Internet addresses given in the Further Reading section to look at Shakespeare's manuscripts, or aquire a scholarly edition of a Shakespeare play (the Arden and the Penguin Shakespeare are good). Find five examples of points in the text where a modern editor has had to choose from so-called 'variant readings'. Try to find examples where the choice has a direct effect on the meaning.

Writing about context

The important thing to remember when writing about context is that the text you are studying should always be your main focus. An essay about Church Doctrine in the Renaissance may be very intelligent and interesting, but may suggest you are studying the wrong subject: similarly, phrases like '*Othello* can tell us a great deal about the Elizabethan attitude towards blackness . . .' show that a student has got the wrong end of the stick, as you should not approach literary works as historical source documents, but as individual works of art. Context should help our understanding of the text, not vice-versa.

ACTIVITY 55

Key skills: information technology – research

1 Choose one of your set texts (other than *Othello* or *Faustus* if you study either of them) and use the Internet addresses in the Further Reading section to research some of the different contexts for it. (As an alternative in a smaller class, work in pairs with each pair taking a separate type of context.)

Key skills: communication – presentation/writing documents

2 Produce a set of notes *of no more than one side of A4 per context* to be handed in and photocopied as a resource for the rest of your group. Present your findings to the group and evaluate which context had the most relevance to your text and why.

COMMENTARY
To Activity 46

The two lists pair up as follows:

a) = iii) and vi): perception of the Jewish race, perception of war
b) = iv): changed attitudes to conventional forms of behaviour and courting
c) = ii): understanding and belief in the creation of humanity
d) = iii): attitude to other European countries
e) = iii) and i): challenging ideas of role of ruler in the state
f) = i) and v): changed attitudes which challenge patriarchal values.

Chapter review

In this chapter, you have investigated the different types of context that can affect a dramatic text and you have developed the skills to evaluate their relationship to the texts in two case studies.

5 Interpretations

In this chapter, you will consider the different possible interpretations of drama texts available to a modern audience, including:

- formalism
- structuralism
- Marxism
- feminism.

You will remember that in the last chapter you looked at a complete dramatic text, Harold Pinter's *Request Stop*, searching for clues as to its meaning at various points in your reading process. As we discussed in the last chapter, the clues which you will have been looking for will have been contextual ones – but you will also have been developing your own ideas as to the meaning of the text, in the absence of any 'authoritative' comment (from a teacher/textbook/critic). In a way, no authoritative comment is needed: what you find in a text *is* the text, particularly in one as enigmatic as *Request Stop*. As Harold Pinter said in the opening quotation of this book, 'Everything to do with the play is in the play.' It is your job to read it, and to interpret it – Assessment Objective 4 states that you must **articulate independent opinions and judgements** – and your interpretation of the text will be an individual one, which may differ to that of others.

However, the assessment objectives also state that your interpretation should also be **informed by different interpretations of literary texts by other readers.** You will need to consider the views of others in forming your own judgements. Quite who these 'others' are, we will discuss later in the chapter.

ACTIVITY 56

On your own answer the following questions as quickly and as honestly as you can.

1 What is your gender?
2 What is your ethnic origin?
3 What is your social class (if you believe in social class)?
4 Which political party would you vote for?
5 Do you think that the feminist movement has made society a better place?
6 What do you see here, a duck or rabbit?

Ways of reading

You may have answered questionnaires in the past without ever really thinking about what they say about you as an individual; however, your answers to the last six questions will have revealed a considerable amount about your background, experience, attitudes and beliefs. When you read a text, you bring to it all of these different aspects and many more: a text concerning an accident involving a dog would have a very different effect on you depending on whether you were an animal lover or held a phobia towards dogs! In this way, a text does not come pre-packaged with meaning – you have your own individual 'way of reading' texts which can also create meaning. This is probably what Pinter meant when he said 'The play exists now apart from you, me or anybody': it has as many meanings as audiences and readers. Common-sense tells us that a writer has an intention of meaning when they write, but whether the audience takes this meaning is a different issue entirely.

This demonstrates the fact that reading is an active experience – you don't just passively receive information, but interpret it and react. Whether you initially saw the duck or the rabbit is a famous illustration of this – the same stimuli can produce a different interpretation from different people. That said, once it has been pointed out to you that the same drawing can be seen either as a duck or a rabbit, you can usually see them simultaneously. Similarly, in responding to a text you can hold your own interpretation and consider someone else's at the same time.

Drama in performance

So far in this chapter, we have been describing reading as a two-way process, a meeting point between what the writer intended and our own personal interpretation of that meaning. However, as usual, the dramatic text is a different prospect altogether and the number of possible interpretations becomes strikingly larger.

Works of poetry and prose are, by and large, the product of one person's mind attempting to convey meaning and the text arrives with us in the same format as the writer finished it. But we already know that this is something which does not necessarily happen in drama. In Chapter 3, the dramatic text was described as a working document which only reaches completion in performance; and in Chapter 4 we considered the way in which different contexts for performance can produce potentially different meanings. However, even in an individual performance the possibility for multiple interpretations exists. A director, in deciding to put on a production of a specific play, will usually have their own ideas about the way the play should be presented and acted. Add to this the fact that the actors will also interpret their own lines in specific ways (and then there are the set and costume designers . . .) and we realise that the interpretation of a play for performance is a multiple effort, and that although the words may be the same, often no one performance is the same as the next. In this way, drama texts can be seen as democratic and open – we do not just have to follow one meaning dictated by a God-like author.

Obviously, we are talking here usually about small differences of interpretation which do not necessarily change our understanding of the overall meaning of the play. Our interpretations of most plays will remain roughly the same. However there are some clear examples where interpretations are decidedly different.

Richard II – twice

A perfect recent example of the way in which plays can be interpreted differently in performance is the two different versions of Shakespeare's *Richard II* which were performed simultaneously in Spring 2000, with Sam West and Ralph Fiennes both playing Richard, one in the RSC production, one at the Gainsborough Studios.

Richard II presents the downfall of King Richard, who is arrogant and impetuous and ignores all advice in treating his subjects poorly. The crisis point arises when he banishes and disinherits young Henry Bolingbroke. When Bolingbroke's father dies and Richard seizes his wealth, Bolingbroke returns to England and seizes the crown, backed by public support. The play ends with Richard's murder, alone in a cell.

From this very brief summary, it may seem that Richard deserves his downfall and that we can have little sympathy for him. However, this is not necessarily the case, and the fact that two productions could exist at the same time demonstrates the way the play can be interpreted in different ways:

Pimlott (the RSC director) thinks the two productions will invite critical comparison, but is convinced it's not a title fight. 'There's room for a thousand productions,' he says, wildly. 'The play is so rich. Each version is through the perspective of those performing it.'

West will apparently play a king miscast, a man upon whom power rests uneasily. The RSC version starts at the Other Place in Stratford, an intimate space which, according to Pimlott, allows the company to perform *Richard II* 'in camera'. By contrast, Fiennes will be a harder king, a flawed but strident character – reflective, but not a wuss. And the Gainsborough Studios, refitted at a cost of £700,000, provide a much bigger stage for him to stalk.

(*Evening Standard*, Wednesday 22 March, 2000)

ACTIVITY 57

Key skills: communication – discussion

What does the extract from the *Evening Standard* suggest about

a the different interpretations of Richard

b the importance of the acting space in the actors' portrayals?

COMMENTARY Notice here not just the obvious point that the two actors will interpret the role differently, but that the set also influences their interpretation. The 'intimacy' of the RSC space encourages West's King, 'on whom power rests uneasily', whereas the bigger stage of the Gainsborough Studios lends itself to a character who 'stalks' and is 'reflective, but not a wuss.' The play focuses on the downfall of King Richard, deposed and finally murdered after a self-indulgent, despotic reign, so our perception of his character is a very important aspect of our understanding it.

In a review of the two plays in *e: the A Level English Magazine*, student Vicki Craighill wrote that 'Samuel West depicted Richard as an emotional wreck, a belligerent, petulant, wilful child with the power to destroy lives', whereas Ralph Fiennes' Richard was a 'shallow, spoilt young man who only began to understand that he was responsible for his own downfall when it was tragically too late.' The two actors' interpretations are clearly similar to a certain extent, although it is interesting that Fiennes' performance emphasised the ultimate tragedy of what happened to Richard.

Sam West as Richard II.   Ralph Fiennes as Richard II.

ACTIVITY 58

**Key Skills: communication –
reading/discussion**

Read the following extract from *Richard II*, in which Richard is deposed by Bolingbroke. Then, discuss your response to Richard's character in the extract with a partner. Consider whether you agree with either West's or Fiennes' interpretation, or whether you have a different interpretation. Do you think the part of Richard could be played sympathetically here? Some relevant aspects for discussion might be:

- To what extent Richard is displaying genuine grief, or whether he is acting the 'showman'.
- Visually, how the scene might be played to gain the maximum effect.

(Re-enter YORK, with RICHARD, and OFFICERS bearing regalia)

RICHARD: Alack, why am I sent for to a king
    Before I have shook off the regal thoughts
    Wherewith I reign'd? I hardly yet have learned
    To insinuate, flatter, bow and bend my knee.
    Give sorrow leave awhile to tutor me
    To this submission. Yet I well remember
    The favours of these men. Were they not mine?
    Did they not sometime cry 'All hail!' to me?
    So Judas did to Christ. But he, in twelve,
    Found truth in all but one: I, in twelve thousand, none.
    God save the king! Will no man say amen?
    Am I both priest and clerk? Well then, amen.
    God save the king! Although I be not he:
    And yet, amen, if heaven do think him me.
    To do what service am I sent for hither?
YORK: To do that service of thine own good will
    Which tired majesty did make thee offer:
    The resignation of thy state and crown
    To Henry Bolingbroke.
RICHARD: Give me the crown. Here, cousin, seize the crown.
    Here, cousin,
    On this side my hand, and on that side thine.
    Now is this golden crown like a deep well
    That owes two buckets, filling one another,
    The emptier ever dancing in the air,
    The other down, unseen, and full of water.
    That bucket down and full of tears am I,
    Drinking my griefs, whilst you mount up on high.
BOLINGBROKE: I thought you had been willing to resign.
RICHARD: My crown I am, but still my griefs are mine.
    You may my glories and my state depose,
    But not my griefs; still am I king of those.
BOLINGBROKE: Part of your cares you give me with your crown.
RICHARD: Your cares set up do not pluck my cares down.
    My care is loss of care, by old care done;
    Your care is gain of care, by new care won.
    The cares I give, I have, though given away,
    They 'tend the crown, yet still with me they stay.
BOLINGBROKE: Are you contented to resign the crown?
RICHARD: Ay, no; no, ay; for I must nothing be.
    Therefore no 'no', for I resign to thee.
    Now, mark me how I will undo myself.

I give this heavy weight from off my head,
And this unwieldy sceptre from my hand,
The pride of kingly sway from out my heart;
With mine own tears I wash away my balm,
With mine own hands I give away my crown,
With mine own tongue deny my sacred state,
With mine own breath release all duteous oaths;
All pomp and majesty I do forswear;
My manors, rents and revenues, I forgo;
My acts, decrees and statutes I deny.
God pardon all oaths that are broke to me,
God keep all vows unbroke are made to thee!
Make me, that nothing have, with nothing griev'd
And thou with all pleas'd, that hast all achiev'd.
Long may thou live in Richard's seat to sit,
And soon lie Richard in an earthy pit.
God save King Henry, unking'd Henry says,
And send him many years of sunshine days!
What more remains?

Richard II, Act IV, sc. i, ll. 162–221

Other readers

Earlier in the chapter, we discussed the part of the assessment objective which stated that your interpretation had to be **informed by different interpretations of literary texts by other readers.** But what exactly does this mean?

ACTIVITY 59

Key skills: communication – discussion

In a group, produce a list of all the different 'other readers' who could possibly affect your interpretation of a literary text. Next, number them in order of importance, making sure you reach a group consensus.

COMMENTARY Although Harold Pinter suggested that 'the comment, the slant, the explanatory note' existed 'in the play', the fact is that we are influenced by a number of people in our understanding of a literary (and in this case dramatic) text, at different levels of complexity and at different points in the process of dealing with the text. The following extract from Tom Stoppard's play *The Real Inspector Hound* presents one kind of 'other reader' in the guises of Birdboot and Moon, two over-enthusiastic theatre reviewers.

BIRDBOOT: It is at this point that the play for me comes alive. The groundwork has been well and truly laid, and the author has taken the trouble to learn from the masters of the genre. He has created a real situation, and few will doubt his ability to solve it with a startling denouement. Certainly that is what it so far lacks, but it has a beginning, a middle and I have no doubt it will prove to have an end. For this let us give thanks, and double thanks for a good, clean show without a trace of smut. But perhaps even all this would be for nothing were it not for a performance which I consider to be one of the summits in the range of contemporary theatre. In what is possibly the finest Cynthia since the war . . .

MOON: If we examine this more closely, and I think close examination is the least tribute that this play deserves, I think we will find that the austere framework of what is seen to be on one level a country-house weekend, and what a useful symbol that is, the author has given us – yes, I will go so far – he has given us the human condition . . .

BIRDBOOT: More talent in her little finger . . .

MOON: An uncanny ear that might have belonged to a Van Gogh . . .

BIRDBOOT: A public scandal that the Birthday Honours to date have neglected . . .

MOON: Faced as we are with such a ubiquitous obliquity, it is hard, it is hard indeed, and therefore I will not attempt to refrain from invoking the names of Kafka, Sartre, Shakespeare, St Paul, Beckett, Birkett, Pinero, Pirandello, Dante and Dorothy L Sayers.

BIRDBOOT: A rattling good evening out. I was held.

The Real Inspector Hound, Tom Stoppard (1968)

ACTIVITY 60

Key skills: communication – discussion/presentation

1 In pairs, prepare a performance of this extract. Think carefully about how you would imagine the two characters to speak and behave.

2 Perform to the class. Then, discuss what the performance suggests about the characters. What is Stoppard saying about theatre reviewers, perhaps?

COMMENTARY

Stoppard's presentation of Birdboot and Moon here is clearly satirical, ranging from their statement of the obvious ('it has a beginning, a middle and I have no doubt it will prove to have an end') to their pompous language ('ubiquitous obliquity', whatever that means) and ridiculous overstatements. The irony, of course, is that these characters are appearing in a play which will no doubt be reviewed. Part of the extract's satire comes from the fact that reviewers can have so much sway; their 'opening night reviews' are often anticipated with dread, as they can make or mar a performance's success, depending on whether they recommend it or not – an example of a very powerful 'other reader'. Maybe Stoppard is getting his own back here!

ACTIVITY 61

Key skills: communication – research

Look through the national papers or on the Internet to find some reviews of productions.

How similar is their language to that of Birdboot and Moon?

Important as reviewers are, they tend not to affect our understanding of literary texts. Some of the readers you may have listed who do this could be:

- teachers
- other writers

- critics (*not* reviewers)
- other students

All of these can offer potentially different readings of texts which can be equally valid – even your teachers! Likewise, your interpretation can be as valid as that of any other reader, providing your comments are sensible and you are able to back them up with evidence from the text. There is no 'right answer' in English Literature, although you must beware of making far-fetched or unsubstantiated interpretations. Critical works which discuss an individual text or author can prove useful in providing alternative viewpoints, although it is worth remembering Pinter's point that 'everything to do with the play is in the play', and that you will be assessed on your **independent opinions**, so there is no point simply copying out chunks from a critical work. By all means read criticism to offer ideas – but remember that it is your ideas that count.

ACTIVITY 62

Key skills: communication – discussion/writing documents

Take a text both you and a partner both know and have studied – it doesn't necessarily need to be dramatic – and then:

1 On your own, choose one of the characters you reacted strongly to, whether for positive or negative reasons. Write as much as you can about your response to the character.
2 Now discuss your responses with your partner. Did they differ in any ways? Are there any points you disagree on? Even if your responses were the same, consider if there are any other ways of looking at it that you may not have considered – if possible, try to take opposing views in your responses. It doesn't matter if you don't really believe the stance you are taking – seeing a possible alternative approach is an important skill to develop.

ACTIVITY 63

Key skills: communication – discussion/presentation

Another useful way of seeing how characters can be perceived in different ways is through hotseating. One member of the class should pretend to be a villain from a literary text – for example, Macbeth, or Alec D'Urberville – and must try to justify their actions to the group. The group can then question them. This often reveals different ways of perceiving someone's behaviour.

ACTIVITY 64

Key Skills: communication – reading/sources

Take the same text as you discussed for Activity 62, and read some critical work on it, whether it is from a book or the Internet. Decide whether there are any aspects of the critical work which you

a agree with
b disagree with.

Share your ideas with a partner.

Theoretical approaches

Whereas the focus of some critics is on individual works or authors, some writers instead focus on specific approaches which they apply to a number of different texts, although in reality they also tend to choose specific texts which best fit their approach. Just as you previously created your own 'blue print' for your individual way of reading when you answered the questions about yourself, these critics have a 'way of reading' in which they are particularly interested in a specific aspect of literature – their 'literary theories.' These theories are often borrowed from other academic disciplines such as philosophy, psychology, sociology and linguistics, and the writers often do not focus on specific texts at all, but instead write about general issues surrounding language, society and the production and reception of literature. Their writing is often highly complex and difficult, and so-called 'schools' of criticism – where a number of writers take broadly the same approach to literature – often contain 'dissenting' or contradictory voices. Any attempt to give a brief account of these schools of criticism inevitably involves over-simplification and will probably misrepresent the view of any one particular critic's approach. However, an understanding of some of the main principles of these different approaches can help you in your interpretations of text and so the task is a worthwhile one. What follows, then, is a brief summary of the main theoretical approaches to literature, with case studies demonstrating their particular application to drama. If you want to explore the complexities of any or all of these theories in more detail, the Further Reading section at the end of this book will offer advice.

WARNING!

Remember that these critical theories are to help you in your response to texts. They should never replace your ideas, and they should also never replace the text itself, which should always be your main focus!

The different theoretical approaches can broadly be defined as taking three angles:

- linguistic
- social
- historical.

Linguistic theories

These approaches to literature are most concerned with language and form, and the way they create meaning. They consider such philosophical questions as the nature of language, how it creates meaning and how language in literature is different from language in everyday life.

Formalism

The Formalists were a group of Russian theorists writing at the beginning of the twentieth century. As their name suggests, they were interested in the nature of literary *form* and the way it created meaning; and although later formalists modified their approach, Formalism is most famous for the radical approaches of writers like Viktor Shklovsky and Roman Jakobson, who considered the form of a piece of writing to be far more important than the content – even to the extent that the content of a piece of writing was an excuse for the production of a literary form: literature is 'the sum total of all stylistic devices employed', according to Shklovsky. Therefore, a Formalist approach to drama would be one which disregards plot and characters and instead focuses purely on aspects of dramatic form and convention. Rather than focusing on the character of the king in *King Lear*, for example, it would consider the ways in which the play evokes the form of the morality play, or its use of traditional conventions of disguise and soliloquy.

Formalism also considered there to be a significant difference between everyday language and the language of literature. Shklovsky defined the term 'defamiliarisation' to refer to the way that literature takes language, normally used purely as a means of communication, and refreshes our view of it by presenting it in a strikingly different way. Literature's task is to present things to us in an entirely new light. One of the ways of doing this is known as 'baring the device.' This refers to the way in which literature reveals and emphasises those aspects of its technique that would normally be hidden, in order to shake the reader/audience from many of their assumptions about the text.

Because Formalism is a very extreme way of looking at texts, it is rarely used nowadays as an approach to most literature. However, of all the genres of literature, it still has the most to offer in its analysis of drama, as so many plays do 'bare the device' and play with the conventions of theatre. When Tennessee Williams has Tom come on to declare 'I am the narrator of the play, and also a character in it' in the extract from *The Glass Menagerie* in Chapter 3, as well as explaining 'the fiddle in the wings' by saying 'In memory, everything seems to happen to music', he is drawing attention to the *performative* aspects of the piece of drama and the conventions that go with it. The way in which so many modern plays reveal their performative aspects owes much to the work of Bertolt Brecht.

Bertolt Brecht and the 'alienation effect'

By far the most famous and influential dramatist to 'bare the device' is the German dramatist Bertolt Brecht (1898–1956), whose concept of *Verfremdungseffekt*, the 'alienation effect', was very similar to that of 'defamiliarisation' and 'baring the device'. Brecht considered that theatre had two primary functions – to instruct and to entertain. However, he felt that in naturalistic drama, the two functions got in each other's way: if an audience were being entertained, this was normally by means of an emotional, rather than an intellectual, reaction as the audience empathised with the characters on the stage. Brecht felt that this was not the effect that drama should be having, and proposed that measures should be taken to remind the audience that what they were watching was a constructed piece of artistry, to enable them to reflect on the purpose of the drama, and so be instructed by it: 'I am forced here simply to state our belief that we can indeed encourage artistic understanding on the basis of alienation'.

The typical Brechtian performance is one which constantly emphasises the fact that actors are playing roles (by having males taking female roles, for example, or playing more than one character), as well as drawing attention to incidental aspects of the performance (by having the actors change onstage, or the musicians in a very visible position). When Caryl Churchill writes, in her introduction to her play *Cloud Nine* (1983), that 'Betty, Clive's wife, is played by a man because she wants to be what men want her to be, and, in the same way, Joshua, the black servant, is played by a white man because he wants to be what whites want him to be' then she is very much writing in the tradition of Brechtian 'alienation'.

ACTIVITY 65

Key skills: communication – reading

Take a play which you have studied or are studying (it does not necessarily have to be written after Brecht was writing).

a Identify any aspects of it which are non-naturalistic, or which could be described as 'baring the device'.
b What purpose do these aspects serve in the play? Do they follow Brecht's theory that they allow for greater 'instruction'?

Key skills: communication – writing documents

In groups, choose a scene from a play you are studying (or choose one of the extracts from this book) and rewrite it in a Brechtian fashion, so as to 'bare the devices' in it.

Structuralism and Post-structuralism

Formalism placed emphasis on the form of literary texts; structuralism, as the name suggests, focuses on the structures of literary writing. Structuralists claim that all pieces of literature are only representations of deeper structures which already exist, both on a plot level (for example in fairy stories, which often have similarities of structure, such as 'the saved princess') and on the level of language, which obviously has a grammatical structure, as well as a deep word-pool we draw from. Analysis of plot structure is known as *narratology*. However, it is the structuralist theory of language which has more relevance to the study of drama. Structuralists make the following points about language:

1 All language draws on already existing structures and meanings. Therefore, no utterance is 'original' – it already exists on a deeper level.
2 A traditional view of language would be WORD = MEANING. However, rather than 'word' and 'meaning', structuralists refer to 'signifier' and 'signified' to demonstrate that words are part of an

artificial sign system. Structuralists point out that the relationship between the signifier and signified is complicated, because the relationship between words and their meanings is *arbitrary*. For example, there is nothing dog-like about the word 'dog' and the words 'canine', 'mutt' or 'bitch' could serve the purpose just as well depending on the context.

Structuralism, then, presented language as less than entirely stable, open to misunderstanding and contradiction depending on a person's understanding of individual words. Post-structuralists went one stage further, focusing on this instability and emphasising the difficulties of communication, as mistakes can occur and words can develop contradictory meanings – 'bitch', for example, also has negative connotations and be used as a term of abuse.

Because of the unstable nature of language, they also claimed that writers were not in control of their own medium, language – what they thought they meant could have an entirely different meaning to someone else. That being the case, it is nonsense to talk about what a writer 'meant', or to see texts as reflecting an author's intention. This is what is known as the *plural text*. In many ways, structuralist and post-structuralist theory challenged all our 'common-sense' assumptions about the writing and reading process. But, as Terry Eagleton has written in *Literary Theory: An Introduction*:

The fact that structuralism offends common-sense has always been a point in its favour ... at different times common sense has dictated burning witches, hanging sheep-stealers and avoiding Jews for fear of fatal infection.

ACTIVITY 66

Key skills: communication – writing different documents

In pairs, choose between five to ten words which can have more than one connotation or meaning, and then write a short scene based around some confusion in their use (for example, a scene could be written based around somebody misinterpreting the word 'bitch' in an overheard conversation). The scene can be either comical or serious.

Social theories

Some writers take as their starting-point theories not about literature, but about society, and then apply them to literature. They are interested in what literature has to say about society and its effect on society, largely focusing on the presentation of groups. As an example, the theories we will consider here take as their starting-points firstly the ideas of the political/historical theorist Karl Marx with *Marxist* theory, and then the well-known social movements for equality of the last fifty years with *feminism* and *post-colonialism*.

'Marxist' criticism

Karl Marx (1818–1883) was a German political and social thinker who, along with Friedrich Engels, developed a view of society which remains influential even today. Marx's interests lay in the way in which dominant social groups were formed, kept control and were then superseded. In his most famous work, *The Communist Manifesto* (1848), he claimed that 'the history of all hitherto existing society is the history of class struggles'. Marx held a *dialectical* view of society – that is, he believed that throughout history, society would continue to develop and improve through the struggles of different classes, leading to new dominant groups. Just as the feudal system of the Middle Ages was overtaken by capitalism (a society dominated by ownership of property and production of goods), Marx believed that ultimately capitalism would be overtaken by communism (a society in which everything is shared). This also shows that Marx's view of society was also strongly economic; he believed that people's lives and minds were dictated by their social and economic position and not the other way around, as was traditionally thought.

Although Marx was writing in the nineteenth century, it wasn't until the twentieth century that his theories about society were applied to literature. Although a broad generalisation, we can say that Marxist critics were interested in the way in which different types of literature displayed class struggles; the way in which people were presented as interacting with, and being affected by, their environment; and the means by which the ruling class keep the inferior class 'in their place' through convincing them it is for their own good – known as *ideology*.

ACTIVITY 67

Key skills: communication – discussion

England has recently been referred to as a 'classless society'.

1 In groups, list as many works of literature as you can which may in some way be about class, society and social control. They don't have to be written after Karl Marx – if his theory were true, it should be able to be applied to any work of literature from any period.

2 Look back to the description of the history of drama in the twentieth century in Chapter 2. Does it raise any interesting issues about the presentation of class on the English stage?

3 In the light of the answers you have already given, do you think Marxist criticism has a place in today's 'classless society'?

Feminism

Feminism is probably the most easily accessible of the literary theories, for the simple and obvious reason that it links in with a political movement which has a high profile in today's society, and which has an apparently simple objective: the promotion of equal rights for women. However, although its accessibility is an advantage, we must beware of a reductive view of feminist criticism – it has far more specific aims than simply 'promoting equal rights for women.' Feminist politics certainly has a role to play in the theory, but there are specifically literary aspects which the feminist critic looks at. Feminist criticism (and even this is a simplification):

1 Re-assesses and re-evaluates works of literature from a feminist perspective. For example, *The Madwoman in the Attic* by Sandra Gilbert and Susan Gubar is a critical work which considers the theme of madness and female suppression in certain nineteenth century novels;

2 Re-evaluates the so-called 'canon' of Great English Writers (which, in the earlier part of the twentieth century, was predominantly male) by stressing the achievements of women writers;

3 Considers exactly what it means to 'write as a woman'. For example, is there a specifically female way of writing, and to what extent is a woman's experience different from a man's? This form of criticism is known as *gynocriticism* (for an Activity related to this topic, see *Living Literature*, page 85).

ACTIVITY 68

Key skills: communication – discussion

In groups, brainstorm as many authors as you can. Then, consider your list:

- How many are male? How many female?
- Which authors have you studied? Does this demonstrate a gender bias, or not?

Key skills: communication – reading/discussion

Re-read the extracts written by women in this book; *The Busybody* by Susanna Centlivre (page 36), *Owners* by Caryl Churchill (page 69) and *A Taste of Honey* by Shelagh Delaney (page 42). Then discuss whether there is anything that you can identify as being 'feminine' in these pieces. Do they differ in any ways to the extracts by male writers? Do they express a particularly female point of view?

Colonialism and Post-colonialism

Just as feminist criticism relates to a political movement but is also different in its specific aims, so too colonialist and post-colonialist literature has a link with recent movements towards racial equality and greater understanding between different cultures, but also is specific in its interest: it deals with literature surrounding colonisation, defined by the *Oxford English Dictionary* as 'a body of people who settle in a new locality, forming a community subject to or connected with their parent state'. This is usually the colonisation of the Third World by Western countries, and its effect on the people and culture of the colonised country. *Post*-colonialism deals with the period of time after colonisation, although often the two terms are used interchangeably. Writers such as Chinua Achebe and Wole Soyinka have presented the problems of two cultures clashing and the 'mother' culture being suppressed, and Edward Said has shown how history has misrepresented the East to suit racist *discourses* – circulated ideas imposed by those who will benefit – which then justifies colonisation.

Although primarily concerned with the literature of colonisation, the theory can also be applied to older texts. For example, *The Tempest* by Shakespeare has received a colonialist interpretation, with Prospero being seen as the coloniser who suppresses and enslaves the original culture (Caliban) and makes up excuses to justify it. The colonised countries do not necessarily have to be Third World and the suppression does not have to be literal; *Translations* by Brian Friel (1981) deals with the linguistic suppression of Gaelic in Ireland through the translation of Gaelic place-names into English.

Historical theories

There remains a recent, important approach to consider: New Historicism. It is highly unlikely that you will ever use it directly yourself, as it relates to the wider issues of the way in which literature fits into history and how we can use history in our understanding of literature. However, it is important in that it tells us something about historical contexts, an important part of the assessment objectives: for AO5 ii (A2), you will be expected to **evaluate the significance of cultural, historical and other contextual influences** in your understanding of a text.

New Historicism makes two important points which distinguish it from the 'older' historicist view:

1 Unlike older historicist approaches to literature, which saw it as passively floating above history like a privileged cream, new historicism emphasises the *historicity* of the text. Literature is still a historical document, a product of its time, but is also capable of influencing and interacting with history in a dynamic way, rather like the modern media and the debates which rage as to the effects of television violence.
2 History is always a version of the past, rather than the past itself. Therefore, history is also a 'text' and we should be as cautious when reading it as we should when reading, say, a piece of journalism. History is often created within certain discourses, or ways of dealing with specific subjects, which are themselves biased and created by those in power. Edward Said has shown how the historical presentation of the Orient has often suited the racist *ideology* of the scholars who recorded it. (Notice how, with terms such as *discourse* and *ideology*, New Historicism borrows from both Marxist and post-colonialist ideas.)

TERMINOLOGY BOX 3		
Theory	**Approach**	**Key concepts**
Formalism	Focus on crafted aspects of text; emphasis on form above content.	■ Defamiliarisation ■ 'Baring the device'
Structuralism/ Post-structuralism	Structures of plot/language.	■ Signifier/signified ■ Plural text
Marxism	Focus on class conflict and the way economics affect individual lives.	■ Ideology
Feminism	Re-evaluation of literature from a feminist perspective.	■ 'Writing as a woman' ■ Gynocriticism
Colonialism/ Post-colonialism	Suppression of culture by colonists; effect on individual.	■ Discourse
New Historicism	Focus on historicity of the text; text as historical document.	■ Discourse ■ Ideology

Case studies

Theory should never exist on its own, but should always be in response to literature. That being the case, what follows are three case studies demonstrating how different texts might be approached from specific theoretical angles. Make sure that you try the Activities before you read the Commentary, so that you can have some practice dealing with the issues of the different theories

Case Study 1: Post-structuralism
Endgame *by Samuel Beckett and* King Lear *by William Shakespeare*

We said earlier that post-structuralism focused on the instability of language and it could be said that post-structuralists are most interested in those occasions when the usually strong link between a signifier and its signified is severed or confused, creating misunderstanding or contradiction. *Endgame* by Samuel Beckett and *King Lear* by Shakespeare are good examples. Beckett was a writer in the absurdist school of drama in the 1950s (see page 39) and the surrealism of his plays mean that they are ripe for post-structuralist analysis. *Endgame* is an extreme example of this surrealism – it is hard to say what it is about. It is enough to say that the two characters in the extract, Nell and Nagg, live in separate dustbins, appear to be a senile old couple and are the parents of another character in the play, Hamm – apparently!

The extract from *King Lear* is useful in demonstrating that literary theory does not just have to be applied to modern texts – it can be applied backwards to any literary text (or should be able to be, if it is worth its salt). King Lear has given his powers away at the start of the play to two of his three daughters, Goneril and Regan. However, once they have power they ungratefully refused to allow him to stay in their castles and Lear has been thrown out into a howling storm with only his 'Fool' and his disguised serving-man, Kent. There, they meet Edgar, son of the Duke of Gloucester who has been wrongly accused of plotting towards his father's death – and so is disguised as a madman to avoid being captured. Oh, yes – Lear is also sliding towards insanity. As you can imagine, all of this makes for a good deal of linguistic confusion!

ACTIVITY 69

Key skills: communication – reading/discussion

Read the following two extracts and mark all of the different points at which there appears to be confusion. Focus particularly on confusions of language, where meanings are misunderstood – what post-structuralists would consider to be a split between the signifier and signified. When you have finished, share your ideas with a partner.

NAGG: Can you hear me?
NELL: Yes. And you?
NAGG: Yes. *(Pause.)* Our hearing hasn't failed.
NELL: Our what?
NAGG: Our hearing. *(Pause.)* Have you anything else to say to me?
NAGG: Do you remember –
NELL: No.
NAGG: When we crashed on our tandem and lost our shanks.
(They laugh heartily.)
NELL: It was in the Ardennes.
(They laugh less heartily.)
NAGG: On the road to Sedan. *(They laugh still less heartily.)*
Are you cold?
NELL: Yes, I'm perished. And you?
NAGG: I'm freezing. *(Pause.)* Do you want to go in?
NELL: Yes.
NAGG: Then go in. *(Nell does not move.)* Why don't you go in?
NELL: I don't know.
(Pause.)
NAGG: Has he changed your sawdust?
NELL: It isn't sawdust. *(Pause. Wearily.)* Can you not be a little accurate, Nagg?
NAGG: Your sand then. It's not important.
NELL: It is important.
(Pause.)
NAGG: It was sawdust once.
NELL: Once!
NAGG: And now it's sand. *(Pause.)* From the shore.

Endgame, Samuel Beckett (1957)

Enter EDGAR disguised as a madman.

EDGAR: Away! The foul fiend follows me! Through the sharp hawthorn blows the cold winds. Humh! Go to thy bed and warm thee.

LEAR: Didst thou give all to thy daughters?
And art thou come to this?

EDGAR: Who gives anything to poor Tom? whom the foul fiend hath led through fire
     and through flame, through ford and whirlpool, o'er bog and quagmire; that hath laid knives under his pillow, and halters in his pew; set ratsbane by his porridge; made him proud of heart, to ride on a bay trotting horse over four-inch'd bridges, to course his own shadow for a traitor. Bless thy five wits! Tom's a-cold. O! Do de, do de, do de. Bless thee from whirlwinds, star-blasting, and taking! Do poor Tom some charity, whom the foul fiend vexes. There could I have him now, and there, and there again, and there. *(Storm still.)*

LEAR: What? Has his daughters brought him to this pass?
Could'st thou save nothing? Would'st thou give 'em all?

FOOL: Nay, he had reserved a blanket, else we had been all shamed.

LEAR: Now all the plagues that in the pendulous air
Hang fated o'er men's faults and lights on thy daughters!

KENT: He hath no daughters, sir.

LEAR: Death, traitor! Nothing could have subdu'd nature
     To such a lowness but his unkind daughters.
Is it the fashion that discarded fathers
Should have thus little mercy on their flesh?
Judicious punishment! 'twas this flesh begot
Those pelican daughters.

EDGAR: *Pillicock* sat on Pillicock Hill: *pillicock*: thought to be slang for 'penis'
Alow, alow, loo, loo!

KENT: This cold night will turn us all to fools and madmen.

King Lear, Act III, sc. iv, ll 45–77

COMMENTARY   There are a number of clear misunderstandings between Nagg and Nell, often with comic effect:

NAGG: Yes. (Pause) Our hearing hasn't failed.

NELL: Our what?

However, these are not necessarily linguistic confusions. Notice the inability of language to bring about action in the dialogue: Nagg tells Nell 'Then go in', but then *(Nagg does not move).* There is also the confusion surrounding the sand and sawdust, particularly when Nagg says 'It was sawdust once', implying some magical transformation when in actual fact it simply means that the sawdust has been replaced by sand.

As is often the case with Beckett, the entire play encourages a post-structuralist reading, as Beckett's world is one where all of our usual referents in reality: time, place, memory and, most importantly, language, have become unstable. Nell and Nagg's physical deafness and their lack of memory make it very difficult to deal with any 'outside reality', making any meaningful conversation almost impossible. As Vladimir says in Beckett's most famous play, *Waiting for Godot,* 'This is becoming really insignificant.'

The extract from *King Lear* also demonstrates people finding it very difficult to communicate. Shakespeare unusually takes the precaution of giving us a stage direction, '*Storm still*' (meaning the storm continues), and the storm represents just one form of confusion in the scene. There is, most obviously, Edgar's feigned gobbledegook, but also notice that Lear can only understand it in his own terms, assuming 'poor Tom' has been badly treated by his daughters. Lear has to be reminded by Kent that 'He hath no daughters, Sir.' Add to this the Fool's *word-play* (common in Shakespeare and one of the clearest examples of words having different, sometimes confusing meanings) and we have a scene in which words fail to communicate any real meaning successfully. When they do it is a meaning other than the one intended! Little wonder Kent says, 'This cold night will turn us all to fools and madmen'!

Case Study 2: Marxist Theory
John Osborne, Look Back in Anger

Look Back in Anger was first performed in 1956 and was almost immediately recognised as a revolution in British theatre. The main dominating character, Jimmy Porter, was the stereotypical 'angry young man', furious with the world and bitter about his status in it. He is well-educated and intelligent, yet only runs a sweet stall. He is also very class conscious: he is working-class, unlike his upper-middle class wife Alison, whose father was a Colonel in India before moving back to Britain.

ACTIVITY 70

Key skills: communication – discussion

In the following extract, Jimmy attacks Alison verbally about her background and particularly her mother, in the presence of her friend Helena and his friend Cliff.

1 Note down any references Jimmy makes to class, and then discuss exactly what it is about Alison's mother that has so enraged him.

2 Comment on the meaning of the following things Jimmy says:

'Can you 'ear me, mother.'

'she could tell you that this is not down to any dark, unnatural instincts I possess'

'that poor old charger of mine, all tricked out and caparisoned in discredited passions and ideals!'

'Why *don't* we brawl? It's the only thing left I'm any good at.'

3 Discuss the importance of the complicated metaphor of the 'grey mare' at the end of Jimmy's monologue. What does it represent? What is Jimmy's point?

ALISON: *(recognizing an onslaught on the way, starts to panic)* Oh yes, we all know what you did for me! You rescued me from the wicked clutches of my family, and all my friends! I'd still be rotting away at home, if you hadn't ridden up on your charger, and ridden me off!

JIMMY: The funny thing is, you know, I really did have to ride up on a white charger – off white, really. Mummy locked her up in their eight bedroomed castle, didn't she? There is no limit to what the middle-aged mummy will do in the holy crusade against ruffians like me. Mummy and I took one quick look at each other, and, from then on, the age of chivalry was dead. I knew that, to protect her innocent young, she wouldn't

hesitate to cheat, lie, bully and blackmail. Threatened with me, a young man without money, background or even looks, she'd bellow like a rhinoceros in labour – enough to make every male rhino for miles turn white, and pledge himself to celibacy. But even I underestimated her strength. Mummy may look over-fed and a bit flabby on the outside, but don't let that well-bred guzzler fool you. Underneath all that, she's armour plated – *(He clutches wildly for something to shock Helena with)* She's as rough as a night in a Bombay brothel, and as tough as a matelot's arm. She's probably in that bloody cistern, taking down every word we say. *(kicks cistern)* Can you 'ear me, mother. *(sits on it, beats like bongo drums)* Just about get her in there. Let me give you an example of this lady's tactics. You may have noticed that I happen to wear my hair rather long. Now, if my wife is honest, or concerned enough to explain, she could tell you that this is not due to any dark, unnatural instincts I possess, but because (a) I can usually think of better things than a haircut to spend two bob on, and (b) I prefer long hair. But that obvious, innocent explanation didn't appeal to Mummy at all. So she hires detectives to watch me, to see if she can't somehow get me into the *News of the World*. All so that I shan't carry off her daughter on that poor old charger of mine, all tricked out and caparisoned in discredited passions and ideals! The old grey mare that actually once led the charge against the old order – well, she certainly ain't what she used to be. It was all she could do to carry me, but your weight *(to Alison)* was too much for her. She just dropped dead on the way.
CLIFF: *(quietly)* Don't let's brawl, boyo. It won't do any good.
JIMMY: Why *don't* we brawl? It's the only thing left I'm any good at.

Look Back in Anger, John Osborne (1956)

COMMENTARY   Clearly, much of Jimmy's venom is aimed at the fact that Alison's mother did not like him because of his class – 'there is no limit to what the middle-aged mummy will do in the holy crusade against ruffians like me.' She did not consider him good enough for her daughter, something Jimmy refers to ironically in the phrase 'unnatural instincts I possess', as if he is somehow sub-human. Notice the way he also deliberately drops his 'aitch' when pretending to talk to the mother – 'Can you 'ear?' The reference to the romantic idea of the 'charger' (the horse on which the knight would save the distressed damson) is presented ironically by Jimmy as a 'grey mare', perhaps because knights were relatively privileged, whereas Jimmy is very conscious of his working-class status. On the level of class conflict, then, a Marxist interpretation is very appropriate. The grey mare also comes to represent the fight against an old, corrupt order, a strongly Marxist idea, 'caparisoned' (armed and protected) with 'discredited passions and ideals'. Jimmy presents himself as a class warrior against the 'old order' – similar to Marx's ideas of history being created by class struggle – but in this case, the mare cannot carry Alison's weight and dies. Jimmy's ideals have come to nothing, one of the reasons why he can do nothing but 'brawl'.

Case Study 3: Feminism
Henrik Ibsen, **A Doll's House**

When *A Doll's House* appeared on the stage in Ibsen's native Norway in 1879, it caused a storm of controversy: so much so that invitations read, 'You are requested not to mention Ibsen's *Doll's House*'! What was so shocking that Ibsen's play became such a taboo? Well, through telling the story of Nora Helmer and her husband, Torvald, Ibsen portrayed the unequal status of women in the society of the time. The story is as follows:

Nora and Torvald Helmer are married with children in a seemingly happy domestic situation, but there is a secret. Torvald was seriously ill in the past and Nora had borrowed money from one Krogstad to take him away to recover. However, in order to do so, she had to forge her husband's signature (as women themselves were not legally allowed to take loans), something she kept from him by telling him the money had come from her father.

Now, Torvald has a responsible job at the bank and Krogstad has fallen on hard times. He returns from Nora's past, demanding that she persuade Torvald to give him a job, or he will expose her fraud – and destroy the Helmers' reputations. Torvald refuses, and Krogstad reveals the truth to him. Horrified, he condemns Nora as a wife and mother and decides 'the thing must be hushed up at all costs'. Krogstad changes his mind and promises not to expose the fraud and Torvald thinks the family have been saved but, disgusted at the fact that she has been condemned for an act of love, and with Torvald's cowardice in refusing to stand up to Krogstad and accept responsibility, Nora leaves her husband – and her children.

It is this last part of the story that so horrified audiences. For Nora to abandon her husband and children was considered an outrageous act, cruel and unnatural – so much so that Ibsen was pressured into writing an alternative ending (something he felt was a 'barbaric outrage') in which Nora weakly changed her mind at the last minute when presented with her children.

There are clearly very strong feminist aspects to this play. The 'doll's house' which exists at the beginning of the play appears happy, but is one in which Nora is treated as an inferior 'pet' by her chauvinistic husband. By the end of the play, she has reacted against him, rejected the 'doll's house' and asserted her independence. However, although there were those who claimed it for the feminist movement, the general reaction to the play hardly 'appreciated' these feministic aspects and Ibsen himself said 'I must reject the honour of having consciously worked for the woman's cause . . . For me it has been an affair of humanity.' Even so, the play encourages a feminist response and in many ways feminist literary theory has allowed such a response, so that today we can appreciate Ibsen's vision.

Key skills: communication – reading

The following extract occurs just after a fancy-dress party, when Torvald has discovered Nora's secret but has also just discovered that Krogstad will not reveal the fraud. Act out the scene with a partner, and then do the following:

1 Go through the text and find all the aspects of Torvald's speech that are in any way chauvinistic.

2 Nora speaks very little in the extract: discuss why you think this is. How might she act throughout Torvald's speeches? (Clues are given in what he says.)

3 What is the significance of Nora 'taking off this fancy-dress' at this point in the play?

NORA: And me?

HELMER: You too, of course, we are both saved, you as well as me. Look, he sent your IOU back. He sends his regrets and apologies for what he has done ... His luck has changed ... Oh, what does it matter what he says. We are saved, Nora! Nobody can do anything to you now. Oh, Nora, Nora ... but let's get rid of this disgusting thing first. Let me see ... *(He glances at the IOU)* No, I don't want to see it. I don't want it to be anything but a dream. *(He tears up the IOU and both letters, throws all the pieces into the stove and watches them burn.)* Well, that's the end of that. He said in his note you'd known since Christmas Eve ... You must have had three terrible days of it, Nora.

NORA: These three days haven't been easy.

HELMER: The agonies you must have gone through! When the only way out seemed to be ... No, let's forget the whole ghastly thing. We can rejoice and say: It's all over! It's all over! Listen to me, Nora! You don't seem to understand: it's all over! Why this grim look on your face? Oh, poor little Nora, of course I understand. You can't bring yourself to believe I've forgiven you. But I have, Nora, I swear it. I forgive you everything. I know you did what you did because you loved me.

NORA: That's true.

HELMER: You loved me as a wife should love her husband. It was simply that you didn't have the experience to judge what was the best way of going about things. But do you think I love you any less for that; just because you don't know how to act on your own responsibility? No, no, you just lean on me, I shall give you all the advice and guidance you need. I wouldn't be a proper man if it didn't find a woman doubly attractive for being so obviously helpless. You mustn't dwell on the harsh things I said in that first moment of horror, when I thought everything was going to come crashing down about my ears. I have forgiven you, Nora, I swear it! I have forgiven you!

NORA: Thank you for your forgiveness.

(She goes out through the door, right.)

HELMER: No, don't go! *(He looks through the doorway)* What are you doing in the spare room?

NORA: Taking off this fancy dress.

HELMER: *(standing at the open door)* Yes, do. You try and get some rest, and set your mind at peace again, my frightened little song-bird. Have a good long sleep; you know you are safe and sound under my wing. *(Walks up and down near the door.)* What a nice, cosy little home we have here, Nora! Here you can find refuge. Here I shall hold you like a hunted dove I have rescued unscathed from the cruel talons of the hawk, and calm your poor beating heart. And that will come, gradually, Nora, believe me. Tomorrow you'll see everything quite differently. Soon everything will be just as it was before. You won't need me to keep on telling you I've forgiven you; you'll feel convinced of it in your own heart. You don't really imagine me ever thinking of turning you out, or even of reproaching you? Oh, a real man isn't made that way, you know, Nora. For a man, there's something indescribably moving and

very satisfying in knowing that he has forgiven his wife – forgiven her, completely and genuinely, from the depths of his heart. It's as though it made her his property in a double sense: he has, as it were, given her a new life, and she becomes in a way both his wife and at the same time his child. That is how you will seem to me after today, helpless, perplexed little thing that you are. Don't you worry your pretty little head about anything, Nora. Just you be frank with me, and I'll take all the decisions for you ... What's this? Not in bed? You've changed your things?
NORA: *(in her everyday dress)* Yes, Torvald, I've changed.
HELMER: What for? It's late.
NORA: I shan't sleep tonight.
HELMER: But my dear Nora ...
NORA: *(looks at her watch)* It's not so terribly late. Sit down, Torvald. We two have a lot to talk about.

(Henrik Ibsen, *A Doll's House (1879)*, translated by James MacFarlane)

Case Study 4: Colonialism

The following extract is from the play *Death and the King's Horseman* by Wole Soyinka, a play set in Nigeria in the 1940s which explores the cultural clashes brought on by colonisation. The King has died recently and his horseman, Elesin, is about to undergo a ritual in which he will die and accompany the King to heaven. However, the Colonial District Officer, Pilkings, considers this to be against the law and interferes, with disastrous consequences. In the following extract, Pilkings and his wife Jane have been disturbed in their preparations for a fancy dress party by news of the forthcoming ritual, and Pilkings has called his African manservant Joseph to find out more about it.

ACTIVITY 72

**Key skills: communication –
reading/discussion**

Read the following extract, and then consider the following:

1 In what ways does this passage present the incompatibility of the two separate cultures? Think particularly about the discussion regarding Olunde.

2 Is there any sense of an *implied author* in the passage (for a definition of implied author, see page 9)? To what extent is the presentation of Pilkings and Jane positive or negative?

3 What is your reaction to the attitudes displayed by Pilkings?

PILKINGS: Joseph, are you a Christian or not?
JOSEPH: Yessir.
PILKINGS: Does seeing me in this outfit bother you?
JOSEPH: No sir, it has no power.
PILKINGS: Thank God for some sanity at last. Now Joseph, answer me on the honour of a Christian – what is supposed to be going on in town tonight?
JOSEPH: Tonight sir? You mean that chief who is going to kill himself?
PILKINGS: What?
JANE: What do you mean, kill himself?
PILKINGS: You do mean he is going to kill somebody don't you?
JOSEPH: No master. He will not kill anybody and no one will kill him. He will simply die.

JANE: But why Joseph?

JOSEPH: It is native law and custom. The King die last month. Tonight is his burial. But before they can bury him, the Elesin must die so as to accompany him to heaven.

PILKINGS: I seem to be fated to clash more often with that man than with any of the other chiefs.

JOSEPH: He is the King's chief Horseman.

PILKINGS: (*in a resigned way*) I know.

JANE: Simon, what's the matter?

PILKINGS: It would have to be him!

JANE: Who is he?

PILKINGS: Don't you remember? He's that chief with whom I had a scrap some three or four years ago. I helped his son get to a medical school in England, remember? He fought tooth and nail to prevent it.

JANE: Now I remember. He was that very sensitive young man. What was his name again?

PILKINGS: Olunde. Haven't replied to his last letter come to think of it. The old pagan wanted him to stay and carry on some family tradition or the other. Honestly I couldn't understand the fuss he made. I literally had to help the boy escape from close confinement and load him onto the next boat. A most intelligent boy, really bright.

JANE: I rather thought he was much too sensitive you know. The kind of person you feel should be a poet munching rose petals in Bloomsbury.

PILKINGS: Well, he's going to make a first class doctor. His mind is set on that. And as long as he wants my help he is welcome to it.

JANE: (*after a pause*) Simon.

PILKINGS: Yes?

JANE: This boy, he was his eldest son wasn't he?

PILKINGS: I'm not sure. Who could tell with that old ram?

JANE: Do you know, Joseph?

JOSEPH: Oh yes madam. He was the eldest son. That's why Elesin cursed master good and proper. The eldest son is not supposed to travel away from the land.

JANE: (*giggling*) Is that true Simon? Did he really curse you good and proper?

PILKINGS: By all accounts I should be dead by now.

JOSEPH: Oh no, master is white man. And good Christian. Black man juju can't touch master.

JANE: If he was his eldest, it means that he would be the Elesin to the next King. It's a family thing isn't it Joseph?

JOSEPH: Yes madam. And if this Elesin had died before the King, his eldest son must take his place.

JANE: That would explain why the old chief was so mad when you took the boy away.

PILKINGS: Well it makes me all the more happy I did.

JANE: I wonder if he knew.

PILKINGS: Who? Oh, you mean Olunde?

JANE: Yes. Was that why he was so determined to get away? I wouldn't stay if I knew I was trapped in such a horrible custom.

PILKINGS: (*thoughtfully*) No, I don't think he knew. At least he gave no indication. But you couldn't really tell with him. He was rather close you know, quite unlike most of them. Didn't give much away, not even to me.

JANE: Aren't they all rather close, Simon?

PILKINGS: These natives here? Good gracious. They'll open their mouths and yap with you about their family secrets before you can stop them. Only the other day ...

JANE: But Simon, do they really give anything away? I mean, anything that really counts. This affair for instance, we didn't know they still practised that custom did we?

PILKINGS: Ye-e-es, I suppose you're right there. Sly, devious bastards.

Death and the King's Horseman, Wole Soyinka (1975)

Writing about theory: shopping around

The case studies you have just read have looked at specific texts from specific theoretical angles. However, the texts could equally have been approached from different angles; for example, Jimmy's treatment of his wife and their relative status could have received a feminist interpretation; or a new historicist would have been very interested in the relationship between Ibsen's play and the social context. These extracts were also chosen because they encouraged readings from one particular theoretical approach. A Marxist approach works well with *Look Back in Anger,* but not all texts are about class or economics!

What should be very apparent is that no one theory is adequate in explaining all works of literature. One of the problems with literary theories is that they all claim exclusive rights to having 'cracked the code', rather like over-zealous salesmen. However (to use a typically modern, capitalist metaphor, as a Marxist might say) you can afford to shop around – you aren't expected to produce a searing Marxist analysis, or a structuralist deconstruction.

Again, remember that **the theories are there to help you**. They may well give you a foothold in a text, or suggest ideas for exploration. Many of the ideas may have been there anyway – you don't need to be an expert in feminism to realise those aspects in *A Doll's House,* or be a raging Marxist to understand that Jimmy has a 'hang up' about class. What the theories might do, though, is give you a plan of attack in developing your interpretation, and we all know how useful plans of attack are. This chapter's final activity will ask you to use different theories in your response to a text and then to evaluate which were of use – and which weren't.

ACTIVITY 73

Key skills: information technology – research

Choose one of the literary theories outlined above and research it in more detail using the Internet addresses on page 120. Present your findings back to the class.

ACTIVITY 74

Key skills: communication – discussion/making a presentation

1 As a class, read the following monologue, taken from Jim Cartwright's play *Road.* Then, split into four groups and each group take responsibility for one of the following theoretical approaches:

Marxist – looking at class, economic aspects
Formalist – looking at technique and use of language
Structuralist (or post-structuralist) – looking at use of words and shifting meanings
Feminist – looking at the presentation of women.

2 In your groups, attempt to read the extract solely from the perspective of your chosen theory, even if you don't agree with all the points you make. Don't be afraid of making points that seem 'far-fetched'; they can be removed later.

3 Present your ideas back to the whole class

and then discuss which ideas were feasible and made sense. Were any theories better in producing ideas about the text? Did any have no relevance to the extract?

The lights come up on an old armchair, ironing-board and iron. A man is polishing his shoes. The man is middle-aged, soft-spoken, threadbare, with a big hole in his sock.

JERRY: I can't get over it. I can't get over the past, how it was. I just can't. *(He puts his shoes down.)* Oh God, I get these strong feelings inside and they're so sad I can hardly stand it. *(He puts his tie on the ironing board, irons it.)* Oh, oh I can feel one now, it's breaking my heart with its strength and tears are coming in my eyes, and that's just because I thought of something from ago. Oh God. *(He gets down to ironing again.)* Oh they were lovely lovely times though, and such a lilt to them, I go down it when I think. *(He sits down, looking up.)* I hate to mention it, but that big silver ball turning there and all the lights coming off it onto us lot dancing below, and the big band there. And all the lads and girls I knew, all with their own special character. And the way you stood, you know, and you had a cigarette. You even lit a cigarette different then. There was some way, I can't do it now, good thing too, if I could I'd cry me flipping heart out. That's why I never wear Brylcream these days. I can't. National Service too, you did. Everybody did it. You never complained much then, you never felt like complainin', I don't know why. National Service though, you'd all be there. I was RAF, in that soft blue uniform, beret. *(He touches his head.)* When you had a break you'd lie on your bunk, your mate might say, 'Give us a tab'. *(He puts his hands over his eyes.)* And when you went on leave home. To your home town. The weather always seemed to be a bit misty and you'd be walking around familiar streets in your uniform. And everyone would have a little something to say to you. And you'd go to your girlfriend's factory. And they'd send up for her: 'There's a man in uniform to see you.' And you'd wait outside, take your cigs out your top pocket. *(He touches there.)* Light up. Stand there in the misty weather, in your blue uniform. Full up with something. Serving your time. Or you could work for more money in the beginning in a warehouse or by the railway, but it didn't pay off eventually. Or be a fly-boy and sell toys and annuals in the pubs. There was so many jobs then. A lot of people would start one in the morning, finish it, start another in the afternoon, finish it, and go in somewhere else the next day. You had the hit parade. Holidays in the Isle of Man or Blackpool. *'Volare.'* We all felt special but safe at the same time. I don't know. You know I'm not saying this is right, but girls didn't even go in pubs. They didn't. At the dance, in the interval the lads all went in the pub next door. The girls stayed in the dance hall, then afterwards we all came back. And the girls so pretty. Oh when I think of them. *(He puts his hands over his eyes.)* And you went courting in them days. You courted. You walked with them and they had their cardigan over their arm. *(He puts his hand up to his face.)* And the pictures. You went twice, three times a week. The stars, the music, black and white, the kissing. Sex. When I say the word now, and when I said it then it feels different in me. I know it sounds, you know, but it does. I can't get away from the past. I just can't. But no matter what they say. I can't see how that time could turn into this time. So horrible for me and so complicated for me. And being poor and no good, no use. *(He looks up, tears in his eyes.)* I see 'em now me old friends, their young faces turning round and smiling. Fucking hell who's spoiling life, me, us, them or God?

Blackout.

Road, Jim Cartwright (1984)

ACTIVITY 75

**Key skills: communication –
reading/discussion**

Now in the same groups, choose three extracts from this book which you feel lend themselves well to specific approaches. Again, present your ideas to the class.

ACTIVITY 76

**Key skills: communication –
reading/research**

On your own look again at your set drama text and consider different interpretations of it. Are there different ways of looking at it? Would any theoretical approaches help in developing an interpretation of it?

The main aim of an A Level course in English Literature is to develop in its candidates the ability to respond to a literary text in an interesting, intelligent and sensitive way, which also means being able to consider alternative approaches and interpretations. Because of its very nature, the drama text should always be able to do this – after all, an audience is made up of a great many different people with different ways of interpreting what is being performed in front of them. Literary theories are some amongst the many possible ways of responding to a text, and if they give you a keyhole into text, a way into a piece of literature that otherwise would have been closed, then they have served a valuable purpose in enhancing your ability to read drama.

Chapter review

In this chapter, you have worked on producing an individual interpretation and then have developed this to consider the views of others, ranging from classmates, teachers and critics, to specific theoretical approaches to literature.

Further Reading

You will find the following resources useful in furthering your knowledge and understanding of drama:

Internet

Aside from individual websites on particular authors you are studying, the following are more general and offer some very good links to materials on drama and literary theory:

http://andromeda.rutgers.edu.~jlynch/Lit/ (Literary Resources on the Net)
www.britishliterature.com
http://vos.ucsb.edu (Voice of the Shuttle)
http://englishlit.about.com/arts/englishlit (part of About.com)

General

Considering Drama by John Shuttleworth and Andrew Mayne (Hodder and Stoughton)
Living Literature by Frank Myszor and Jackie Baker (Hodder and Stoughton)
Doing English by Robert Eaglestone
e: the A Level English Magazine (Simon Powell Publications)

Chapter 2: Backgrounds to Drama
A History of English Literature, by Alastair Fowler (Oxford)
History of the Theatre by Oscar G. Brockett (Simon and Schuster)
A Chronology of English Literature (York Handbooks) by Martin Gray (Longman)
Drama through the Ages by Mary Berry and Michael Clamp (Cambridge)

Chapter 4: Contexts for Drama Texts
Obviously, the contextual information you are looking for will depend on the author you are studying. There are some general guides to the history of literature which cover the period you are dealing with; *The New Pelican Guide to Literature* (Penguin) and *The Context of English Literature* series (Methuen) are good. The following books are useful for the contexts of Renaissance drama and Shakespeare:
The World of Shakespeare and his Contemporaries, by Maurice Hussey (Heinemann)
Shakespeare: Texts and Contexts, edited by Kiernan Ryan (Open University)

Chapter 5: Interpretations
The following are very useful guides to Theory:
A Reader's Guide to Contemporary Literary Theory, by Raman Selden and Peter Widdowson (Simon and Schuster)
Practising Theory and Reading Literature by Raman Selden and Peter Widdowson (Simon and Schuster)
Beginning Theory by Peter Barry (Manchester University Press)
Literary Theory: An Introduction by Terry Eagleton (Oxford)
For those who are ambitious enough to read some of the theorists' own works, there is a good selection in:
Twentieth Century Criticism: A Reader, edited by David Lodge (Longman)
Modern Theory: A Reader edited by David Lodge (Longman)